Sake, Mirin, and *Dashi stock* are essential to Japanese Cooking.

* *Sake* (rice wine) mellows food, tones down raw taste or smells and improves flavor.
  Dry sherry can be a substitute for *sake.*
* *Mirin* (sweet cooking rice wine) is used to improve flavor and give food glaze and sweetness. *Mirin* may be substituted with 1 Tbsp *sake* and 1 tsp sugar.
  Both *sake* and *mirin* are now manufactured in the USA.
* For preparations of *Dashi stock*, see inside back cover page.

INARI-ZUSHI

OSHI-ZUSHI & BOU-ZUSHI

FANCY SUSHI

SIMPLE KOBACHI & SUIMONO

SUSHI RICE

The standard amount of sushi rice for a general family is 3 or 4 cups. Take into consideration that rice roughly doubles when cooked.

INGREDIENTS

3 CUPS RICE (for 6~7 cups sushi rice)		4 CUPS RICE (for 8~9 cups sushi rice)	
3 cups rice	Vinegar mixture	4 cups rice	Vinegar mixture
3 cups water	6 Tbsp vinegar	4 cups water	9 Tbsp vinegar
3 Tbsp sake	2 Tbsp sugar	4 Tbsp sake	3 Tbsp sugar
3″ (8 cm) square	2 tsp mirin (sweet sake)	4″ (10 cm) square	1 Tbsp mirin (sweet sake)
kombu (kelp)	2 tsp salt	kombu (kelp)	1 Tbsp salt

● You may change the ratio of the vinegar mixture as you like.
● The sushi in this book uses the sushi rice given above unless otherwise specified.

1 Choose high quality rice and wash quickly 30 minutes before cooking.

★Good sushi depends on the right choice of rice. Avoid newly harvested rice, which becomes sticky when cooked. Select rice which has been stored at least three months after harvest. It is best to ask for a rice dealer's advice.

★Wash the rice in a zaru (fine mesh basket) put in a bowl so that broken rice pass through. Since rice absorbs water, it is important to wash quickly. A zaru is suited to this purpose.

1 Stir quickly and discard water.

2 Wash about 30 times in a small amount of water.

3 Stir quickly and discard water.

4 Repeat (3) until water becomes clear.

5 Clear water.

6 Strain water and let stand 30 minutes.

2 Cook rice in the kombu-stock with sake added and allow it to steam for 10 minutes.

★Wipe kombu clean with cloth and score it to enhance flavor. In a rice cooker put specified amount of water and the kombu, and let it stand for an hour (two hours in winter) before cooking.

★ Remove the kombu, add washed rice and sake and cook as usual and allow to continue to steam for 10 minutes. Sake makes the rice soft. Keep in mind that the quantity of sake is 1 Tbsp for 1 cup rice.

1 Let kombu soak about an hour.

2 Add sake just before cooking.

3 Add rice and cook.

3 Mix rice and vinegar mixture in a handai (wooden rice-cooling tub), and make glossy sushi rice.

★Let the handai soak with water and wipe with dry towel. Before transferring the rice, pour 3 Tbsp vinegar over to prevent the sushi rice from becoming watery.
★Put the vinegar mixture into a pan and heat until sugar and salt dissolved. Take care not to bring it to a boil.

★While the rice is hot, pour over the vinegar mixture, and mix together quickly with vertical cutting movements so that it will not become sticky. While mixing, cool with a fan or cardboard, until it reaches body temperature.

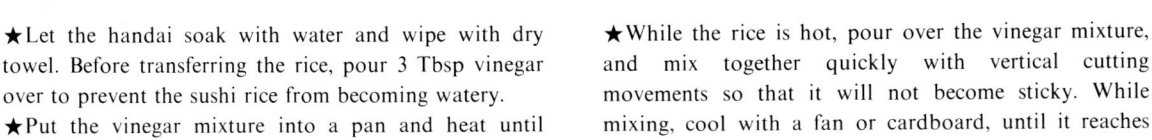

1 Let the handai soak with water.

2 Wipe with dry towel.

3 Pour vinegar over.

4 Heat the vinegar mixture.

5 Pour over.

6 Mix with cutting movements.

7 Fan to cool.

8 Cover with wet towel.

HANDAI AND ITS MAINTENANCE

●The handai (wooden rice-cooling tub) is indispensable for making good sushi. The wood absorbs extra water and gives the rice the proper texture and gloss. Use a larger one. When it is unavailable, a vat or bowl will do.

●Care after it is used is important. Wash well and dry completely. Wrap in paper and keep it with the face downward.

CHIRASHI-ZUSHI
(Scattered Sushi)

With various ingredients arranged attractively on top, chirashi-zushi gives you a gorgeous meal. Make plenty so that you can share it with your friends.

The best sushi for a special occasion.

GOMOKU-ZUSHI (Five-Flavor Sushi)

INGREDIENTS (pp.6-7)

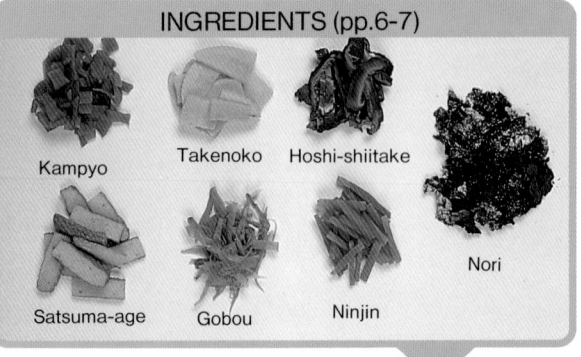

Kampyo   Takenoko   Hoshi-shiitake

Satsuma-age   Gobou   Ninjin   Nori

POINT: Ingredients should be mixed when the sushi rice reaches body temperature. Cooled rice is hard to loosen and ingredients are not mixed evenly, so you should prepare all the ingredients before the rice is cooked.

GARNISH (pp.8-9)

Kinusaya   Saimaki-ebi

Renkon   Kinshi-tamago

1

Add 3 Tbsp white sesame to the sushi rice (pp.2-3).

2

Drain all ingredients and spread them over the rice.

3

Turn over the rice and roughly mix.

4

Mix with a spatula making cutting motions.

5

Transfer all to a container and top with garnish.

Method, pages 6~9

5

INGREDIENTS FOR GOMOKU-ZUSHI (Mixtures)

HOSHI-SHIITAKE (Dried Shiitake Mushroom)

Method: 1. Break the stems of shiitake and soak them with caps in water. Put a plate as a weight to prevent them from floating.
2. Put all the ingredients except mirin in a pan and cook until the liquid almost has gone. Add mirin to make the shiitake glossy.
3. Remove the ends of the stems. Cut the caps and stems into fine strips.

Ingredients:
6 hoshi-shiitake mushrooms
Broth
   2 cups soaking water
   2 Tbsp sugar
   2 Tbsp sake
   3 Tbsp shoyu (soy sauce)
   1 Tbsp mirin
     (sweet cooking sake)

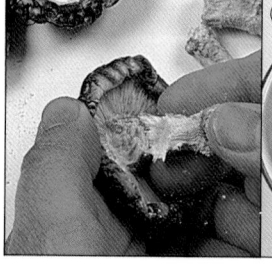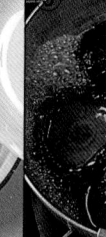

GOBOU (Burdock)

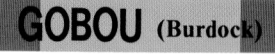

Ingredients:
1⅖ oz (40 g) gobou

Broth
   1 cup dashi stock
   1 Tbsp sugar
   1 Tbsp light shoyu

Method: 1. Wash the gobou with a brush. Shave into flakes and put into water. Change water 2 or 3 times to remove harshness.
2. Boil quickly.
3. Cook in the broth until soft. Drain.

TAKENOKO (Bamboo Shoots)

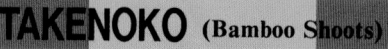

Ingredients:
1¾ oz (50 g) boiled
  takenoko

Broth
   1 cup dashi stock
   2 tsp sugar
   1 Tbsp light shoyu
   1 tsp mirin

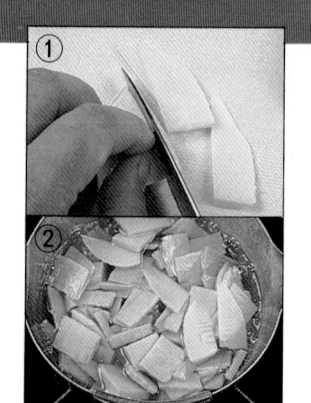

Method: 1. Cut the top part in half. Slice all to the same size.
2. Cook in the broth until seasoned. Drain.
★In the case of canned takenoko, blanch and then cook.

———————————————The ingredients will also be used in other sushi.

KAMPYO (Dried Gourd Shavings)

Ingredients:
⅔ oz (20 g) kampyo
Broth
   2 cups dashi stock
   1½ Tbsp sugar
   1½ Tbsp shoyu
       (soy sauce)
   1 Tbsp mirin

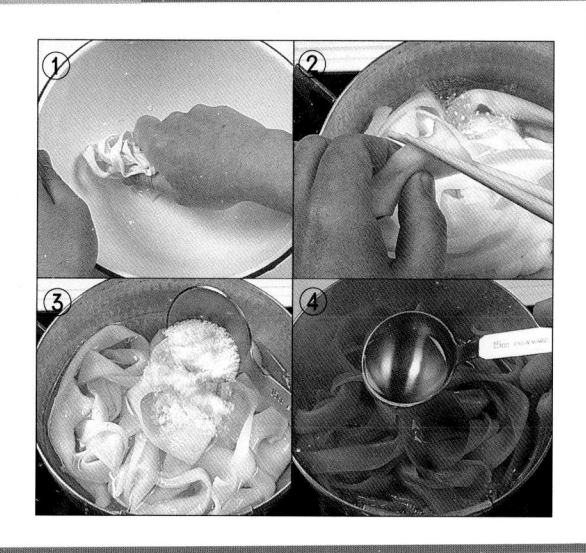

Method: 1. Rinse the Kampyo in water, rub it with salt and wash the salt away.
2. Boil and continue adding water until soft.
3. Cook in the stock and sugar until soft. Add shoyu. When the liquid has evaporated add mirin.
4. Cool and chop roughly into fine pieces.

SATSUMA-AGE (Deep-fried Fish-paste Cake)

Method: 1. Put the satsuma-age on a flat bamboo colander. Pour boiling water over to make less oily.
2. Cut in half and slice.
3. Cook in the broth for a short time. Remove from heat and let it stand.
4. Drain in a colander.

Ingredients:
2 pieces satsuma-age
Broth
   1 cup dashi stock
   1 Tbsp sugar
   1 Tbsp shoyu
   1 Tbsp mirin

NINJIN (Carrot)

Ingredients:
⅓ carrot
Broth
   1 cup dashi stock
   2 tsp sugar
   Dash salt
   1 tsp mirin

Method: 1. Slice the carrot and then cut into sticks.
2. Cook in the broth until soft. Drain.

NORI (Dried Laver)

Tear 1 or 2 sheets of nori to pieces. Wrap in plastic wrap or bag and crush.

SHIRO-GOMA (White Sesame)

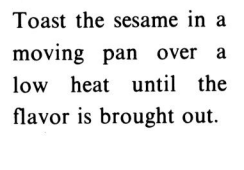

Toast the sesame in a moving pan over a low heat until the flavor is brought out.

INGREDIENTS FOR GOMOKU-ZUSHI (Decorations)

KINSHI-TAMAGO (Shredded Thin Omelet)

Ingredients:
2 eggs
2 egg yolks
Seasoning
   1 Tbsp sugar
   1/5 tsp salt
   1 tsp cornstarch
   (water mixture)
Oil

Method: 1. Break eggs into a bowl. Add egg yolks and seasoning and mix well.
2. Heat a frying pan. Oil pan lightly and pour in (1) and make 5~6 sheets of thin omelets.
3. Cool on the back of bamboo colander. Cut in half and roll up. Shred into fine pieces.

RENKON (Lotus Root)

Ingredients:
5¼ oz (150 g)
         lotus root
Sweetened vinegar
   ½ cup vinegar
   3 Tbsp sugar
   ⅓ tsp salt

Method: 1. Pare the lotus root. Make V-shape cut between holes and slice.
2. Put into the sweetened vinegar. Chop the cut-out parts in (1) into fine pieces and cook together.
3. Boil in vinegared water quickly. When the color changes, transfer to a bamboo colander.
4. Marinate in the well-mixed sweetened vinegar.

Be sure to include three colors, red, yellow and green.

EBI (Shrimp)

Ingredients:

4 shrimps
Sweetened vinegar
½ cup vinegar
2 Tbsp sugar
⅔ tsp salt

Method: 1. Without peeling, devein shrimp. Push through a bamboo skewer from the end.

2. Put 2 Tbsp sake and ½ tsp salt in water which just covers the shrimp, and cook until the color changes red.

3. Remove the head. Peel the shell and cut in half or open the belly.

4. Marinate in the sweetened vinegar. Drain.

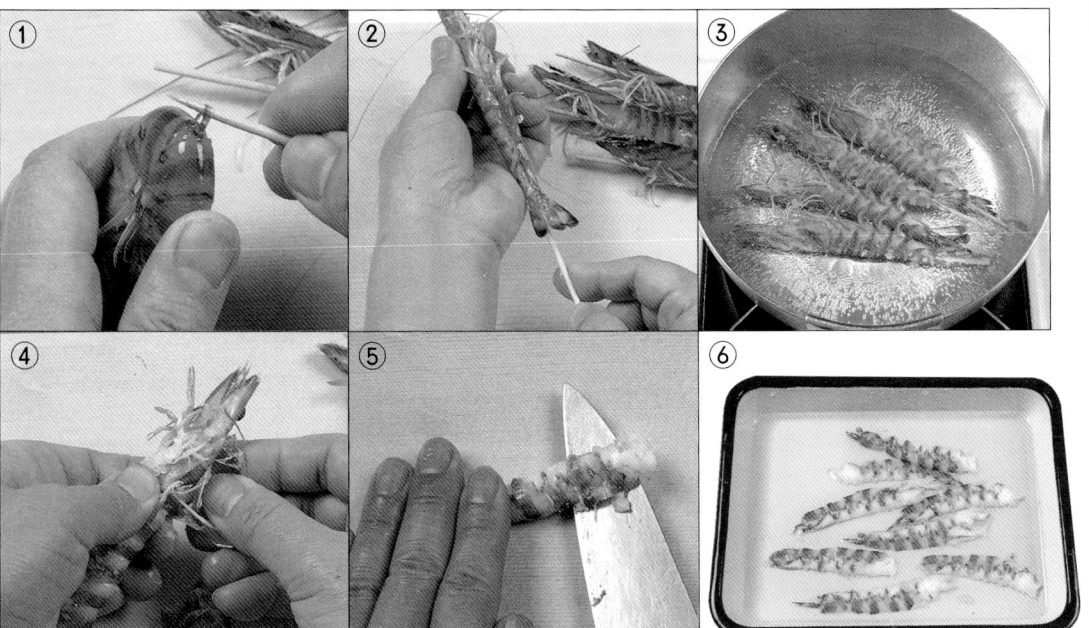

KINUSAYA (Snow Peas)

Method: 1. Remove strings from 12 snow peas. You may leave the tops intact if you like.

2. Boil in salted water. Remove from water when the color changes to bright green. Drain and cut diagonally.

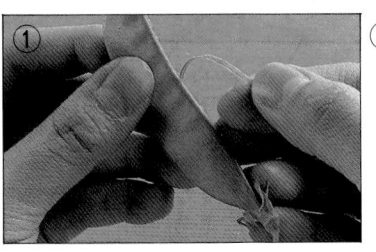

Topped with fresh seafood.

EDOMAE CHIRASHI

Ingredients (4 servings): sushi rice (pp. 2-3, 3 cups rice), $3\frac{1}{2}$ oz (100 g) each of tuna flesh and squid, 8 prawns, $1\frac{3}{4}$ oz (50 g) adductor of round clams, 4 ark shells, 4 Tbsp each of raw sea urchins and salmon roe, thick omelet (3 eggs, 2 Tbsp each of dashi stock and sugar, $\frac{1}{4}$ tsp salt), $\frac{1}{2}$ small cucumber, green perilla, amazu- shouga (p. 64), and wasabi

Method: 1. Prepare the sushi rice as shown on pages 2-3.

2. Cut the tuna and squid into pieces. Shell boiled prawn and cut open as on page 9.

3. Rinse the adductor and ark shells in salted water.

4. Combine the dashi stock and condiments and mix together with eggs to make thick omelet as shown below. Slice the omelet.

5. Cut the cucumber diagonally into slices.

6. Put the sushi rice in a box and top with (2)~(5), sea urchins, salmon roe, green perilla. Add amazu-shouga and wasabi. Dip the pieces in shoyu before eating.

★Tokyo Bay was originally called 'the sea in front of Edo (Tokyo).' The ingredients of this sushi came from Tokyo Bay; thus the name.

★When topped with seafood, it is better to increase the amount of vinegar of sushi rice a little more than usual and decrease the amount of sugar.

THICK OMELET

① Heat and oil the square pan. Remove excess with a paper towel.

② Drop a bit of egg mixture. When it sizzles, it is ready.

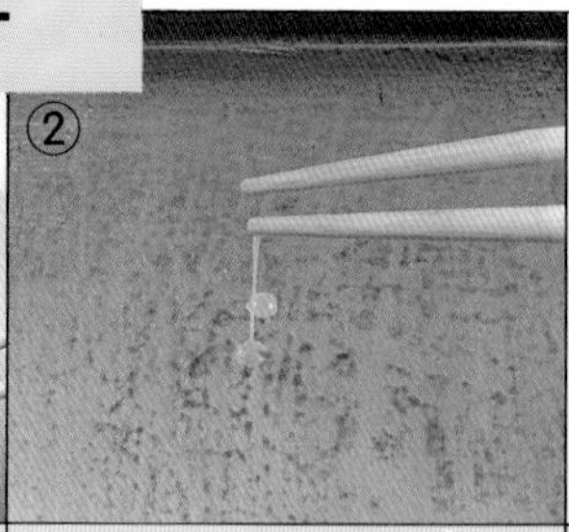

③ Pour in $\frac{1}{3}$ of egg mixture to cover entire pan. When cooked, roll the layer toward you and move it away.

④ Oil the emptied space. Pour in $\frac{1}{2}$ of the rest of egg mixture, even under the layer.

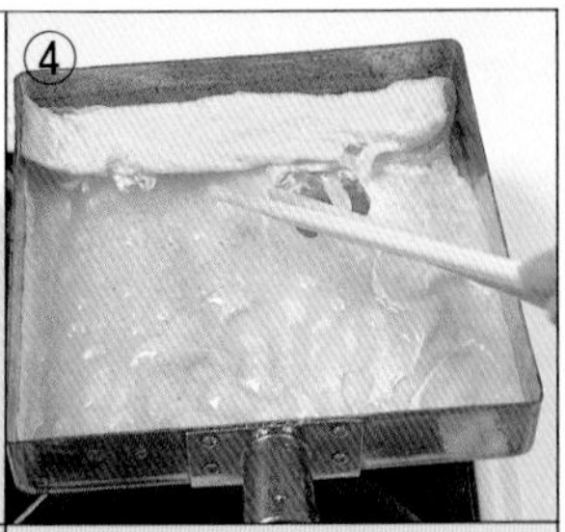

⑤ Roll the layer toward you, and oil the emptied space.

⑥ Move the cooked egg to the other side. Oil the space and add remaining mixture. Cook and roll toward you.

⑦ While hot transfer it to a bamboo mat. Roll it and adjust the form. Put rubber bands on both sides, and let stand until cool. Slice as you like.

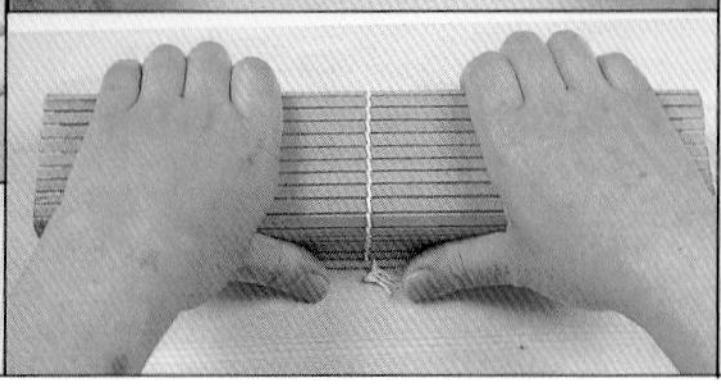

Topped with broiled conger eel.

KANSAI CHIRASHI

Ingredients (4~6 servings): sushi rice 《4 cups each of rice and water, 4″ (10 cm) kombu, 4 Tbsp sake, vinegar mixture (9 Tbsp vinegar, 4 Tbsp sugar, 2 tsp mirin, 1¼ Tbsp salt)》, 3 Tbsp white sesame, 6 dried shiitake (p. 6), ⅔ oz (20 g) kampyo (p. 7), ⅓ carrot (p. 7), 8-12 prawns, 1 broiled conger eel (store bought), 3½ oz (100 g) sea bream seasoned with kombu (store bought), 4-6 Tbsp steamed sea urchin (store bought), 8-12 slices of boiled fish paste, 5¼ oz (150 g) lotus root (p. 8), shredded thin omelet (p. 8), kinome (young Japanese pepper leaves)

Method: 1. Prepare the sushi rice as shown on pages 2-3.

2. See page 6 for dried shiitake. Chop 4 shiitake into fine pieces and slice 2 for decoration. See page 7 for kampyo and carrot.

3. Prepare prawn as shown on page 9 and marinate in the sweetened vinegar. Cut the conger eel and sea bream into bite-sized pieces. See page 8 for the lotus root and shredded omelet.

4. Mix the white sesame with the sushi rice. Add (2) (except shiitake for decoration) and mix well. Transfer all in a bowl and top with the shiitake for decoration, (3), steamed sea urchin, fish paste and scatter the kinome over.

★This is a typical gomoku-chirashi. The sushi rice is sweetened. The main seafood used comes from the Inland Sea of Japan (the Kansai region) and it is cooked or seasoned with vinegar.

The image of a field of flowers.

RAPE BLOSSOM CHIRASHI

Ingredients(4~6 servings): sushi rice(pp.2-3, 4 cups rice), 7 oz (200 g) round clams, (A) 《2 Tbsp each of vinegar and sugar, ½ tsp salt》, 2 bunches of rape blossoms, 2 eggs, (B) 《1 tsp sugar, ⅕ tsp salt》

Method: 1. Prepare the sushi rice as shown on pages 2-3.

2. Rinse round clams in salted water and drain. Combine with the sweetened vinegar (A).

3. Boil rape blossoms in salted water. Sprinkle with a bit of shoyu and squeeze all. Cut into $1\frac{1}{5}''$ (3 cm) pieces.

4. Beat eggs lightly in a pan. Add (B) and make scrambled eggs as shown in the picture.

5. Drain off any excess liquid of (2) and (3). Mix half of each (2), (3) and (4) with the sushi rice. Remove to a large container and scatter the remaining ingredients over.

★The soft taste of scrambled eggs is exquisite. If you prefer more plain taste, reduce the amount of sugar.

RAPE BLOSSOMS

① Sprinkle on rather plenty of salt and rub all lightly.

② Boil quickly and remove to water to cool and drain.

SCRAMBLED EGGS

① Stir well with 4~5 chopsticks. Remove the pan to a wet cloth on and off.

② Use chopsticks and a whisk alternately to get smooth texture.

SPRING

For a poor appetite.

POMPANO CHIRASHI

Ingredients (4~6 servings): sushi rice (pp. 2-3, 4 cups rice), 3 Tbsp white sesame, 4 fresh pompano, ½ cup salt, (A) 《⅓ cups vinegar, 2 Tbsp sugar, ½ tsp salt》, 40 leaves of green perilla, 2 cloves ginger, 6 pieces Japanese ginger

Method: 1. Cut off the head of pompano and clean. Wash and cut into 3 fillets. Remove bones and marinate in the vinegar mixture as shown in the photo. Cut into pieces.

2. Prepare the sushi rice as shown on pages 2-3.

3. Roll about 10 leaves of green perilla and cut into fine strips from the end. Repeat for the rest. Put into water to remove harshness and drain. Cut the ginger and Japanese ginger into fine strips. Put into water and drain.

4. Mix half of the white sesame with the sushi rice evenly. Mix in half each of (2) and (3). Remove to a container and scatter all the remaining ingredients over colorfully.

★The point is to combine plenty of flavorful vegetables, which will get rid of the fishy smell of pompano and give refreshing cool taste.

VINEGARED POMPANO

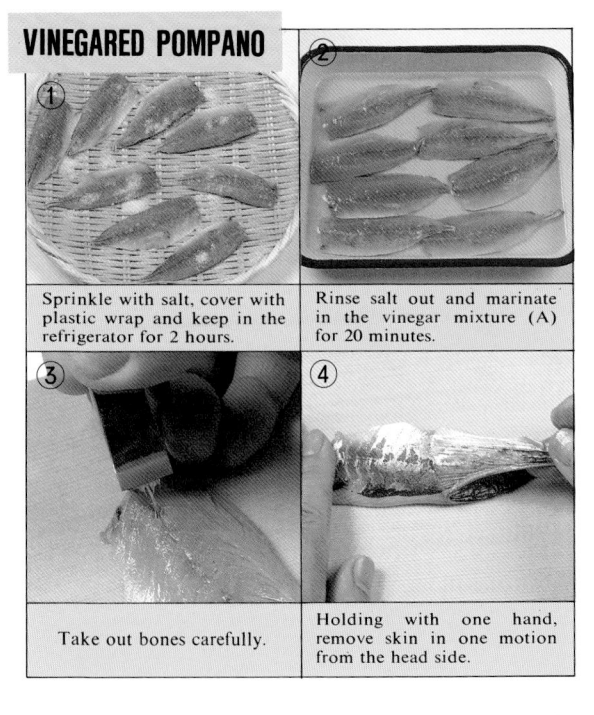

① ② Sprinkle with salt, cover with plastic wrap and keep in the refrigerator for 2 hours.

Rinse salt out and marinate in the vinegar mixture (A) for 20 minutes.

③ Take out bones carefully.

④ Holding with one hand, remove skin in one motion from the head side.

The products of the sea and the countryside.

CHIRASHI OF SALMON AND CHRYSANTHEMUM

Ingredients (4~6 servings): sushi rice (pp. 2-3, 4 cups rice), 10½ oz (300 g) fresh salmon, ½ cup salt,
(A) 《⅓ cup vinegar, 2 Tbsp sugar, ½ tsp salt》,
6 chrysanthemum flowers, 5¼ (150 g) lotus root,
(B) 《½ cup vinegar, 3 Tbsp sugar, ⅓ tsp salt》

Method: 1. Prepare the sushi rice as shown on page 2-3.

2. Place the salmon on a bamboo colander and sprinkle liberally with salt. Keep in the refrigerator for 2 hours. (Or place on dehydrating sheet and sprinkle with 2 tsp salt. Wrap tightly and keep in refrigerator.) Rinse in water and remove salt. Marinate in sweetened vinegar (A) for 30 minutes. Remove skin and cut into pieces.

3. Boil the chrysanthemum flowers as shown in the photo. Marinate in sweetened vinegar mixture (B).

4. Cut the lotus root in half-moon slices, ⅛" (5 mm) thick. Place in vinegared water for some time to get rid of harshness. Cook in vinegared water until the color changes. Drain water and immediately marinate in sweetened vinegar (3) to taste.

5. Mix half each of salmon, drained chrysanthemum flowers and lotus root with the sushi rice. Remove to a container and scatter the remaining ingredients over.

MARINATED CHRYSANTHEMUMS

Boil petals quickly in vinegared water.

Rinse in water, drain and marinate in sweetened vinegar.

FRESH SALMON

Dehydrating sheets are convenient to firm up the fillets of salmon. A bit of salt is enough to remove extra water. The sheet also gets rid of the fishy smell and makes the fish tasty.

Colorful red and white with crab and namasu.

CRAB CHIRASHI

Ingredients (4~6 servings): sushi rice (pp. 2-3, 4 cups rice), 3 Tbsp white sesame, half boiled crab,
(A) 《⅓ cup vinegar, 2 Tbsp sugar, ½ tsp salt》,
7 oz (200 g) white radish, 3⅓ oz (100g) carrot,
(B) 《½ cup vinegar, 3 Tbsp sugar, ⅓ tsp salt》,
1 piece abura-age (fried tofu), 1 clove ginger, ½ bunch mitsuba (honewort)

Method: 1. Prepare the sushi rice as shown on page 2-3.

2. Pull or pick out the crab meat as shown in the photo. Marinate in (A).

3. Slice the radish and then cut into fine strips. Cut the carrot into 1½" (4 cm) lengths and then cut into fine strips lengthwise. Marinate both in (B) to taste. This is called red-and-white namasu.

4. Boil the abura-age quickly to get rid of oil. Cut into fine strips.

5. Cut the ginger into fine strips and put into water.

6. Boil the mitsuba quickly in salted water. Remove into cold water and cut into pieces.

7. Mix the white sesame with the sushi rice evenly. Drain (2)~(6) and mix in half each of them. Remove to a container and scatter all the remaining ingredients over.

★Crabs are said to lower the body temperature, so add ginger to warm the body.

CRABS

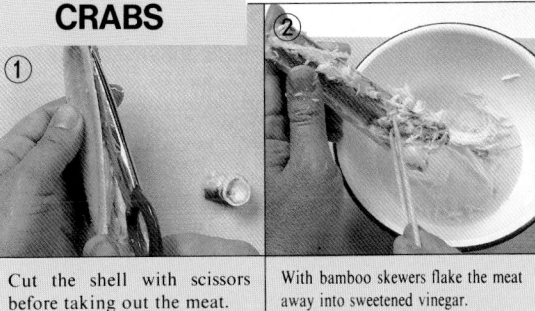

① Cut the shell with scissors before taking out the meat.

② With bamboo skewers flake the meat away into sweetened vinegar.

WINTER

Salad-like WESTERN-STYLE MAZE-ZUSHI

Spanish-style.
SAFFRON-ZUSHI

Ingredients (4 servings): buttered rice 《4 cups rice, ¼ onion, 2 Tbsp unsalted butter, stock (4 cups water + 1 bouillon cube), dash salt and pepper》, (A)《½ cup white wine, 1 tsp saffron》, dressing 《4 Tbsp wine vinegar, 1 Tbsp salt, dash pepper, 3 Tbsp salad oil》, ½ chicken leg, 8 shrimps, 5¼ oz (150 g) short-neck clams, 8 Vienna sausages, 1 tomato, 1 red pepper, 1 Tbsp olive oil, (B)《1 Tbsp white wine, dash salt and pepper》, endive, mint

Method: 1. Buttered rice: Wash rice 30 minutes before cooking, mince onion. Melt butter in a thick pan and fry onion and rice in this order. When the rice turns clear, remove to a rice cooker. Add the stock, salt and pepper, and cook as usual.

2. Heat (A) in a microwave oven (hot) for one minute.

3. Transfer buttered rice (1) to a bowl and add (2) gradually and make colorful. Stir in the dressing and mix well quickly as done for sushi rice (p. 3).

4. Cut the chicken meat into ¾" (2 cm) cubes. Devein and shell shrimp. Wash short-neck clams well. Make diagonal cuts into the Vienna sausages.

5. Place the tomato in boiling water to remove peel and seed. Cut into pieces. Cut the red pepper into thin strips.

6. Heat the olive oil in a frying pan. Add (4) in order and stir-fry. Lastly add (5), stir-frying quickly and season with (B).

7. Mix (6) with (3), and arrange in a container. Tear the endive and scatter over and top with the mint.

Color the rice with heated (A) and mix in the dressing.

Add the ingredients fried with olive oil. Mix well.

Use wine of high quality.
WINE-ZUSHI

Ingredients (4 servings): buttered rice (the same quantity as above), ½ cup red wine (dry), dressing 《4 Tbsp wine vinegar, 1 Tbsp lemon juice, 1 Tbsp salt, dash pepper, 3 Tbsp salad oil》, 1 cuttlefish, 4 slices ham, 1 avocado, juice of ¼ lemon, 8 stuffed olives, 1 Tbsp minced parsley, rosemary

Method: 1. Prepare the buttered rice in the same way as for saffron-zushi.

2. Mix the red wine and the ingredients of the dressing.

3. Transfer buttered rice (1) to a bowl. Stir in (2) and mix quickly.

4. Remove legs from the cuttlefish and clean. Wash well, skin and cut open. Cut into pieces, ⅜" (1 cm) wide and ¾" (2 cm) long. Mince the ham.

5. Cut the avocado in half lengthwise and seed. Cut the half into ⅝" (1.5 cm) cubes, and cut the other half into thin slices. Sprinkle both with the lemon juice. Cut olives into slices.

6. To (3) add (4), avocado cubes, olives and ½ parsley and mix all quickly.

7. Place avocado slices on a platter and add (6). Sprinkle with the remaining parsley and garnish with the rosemary.

Add the red wine to the buttered rice and mix in the dressing.

Add the ingredients and mix all well quickly. Transfer to a platter.

SMALL BOWLS

Good after having a drink or when you feel like eating a bit of something.

CHICKEN SOBORO CHIRASHI

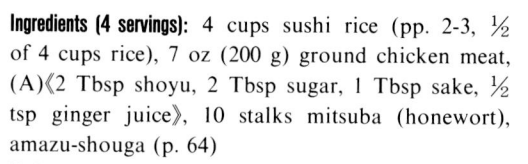

Ingredients (4 servings): 4 cups sushi rice (pp. 2-3, ½ of 4 cups rice), 7 oz (200 g) ground chicken meat, (A)《2 Tbsp shoyu, 2 Tbsp sugar, 1 Tbsp sake, ½ tsp ginger juice》, 10 stalks mitsuba (honewort), amazu-shouga (p. 64)

Method: 1. Prepare the sushi rice (pp. 2-3).
2. Combine the chicken meat and (A) in a pan, and stir-fry over heat. Continue stirring using a few chopsticks until the liquid has almost entirely evaporated. (chicken-soboro)
3. Cut the mitsuba into ¾″ (2 cm) lengths. Cut the amazu-shouga into thin strips.
4. Place the sushi rice in a small bowl. Scatter chicken-soboro over and garnish with the mitsuba and ginger.

★The remaining sushi rice can be used to make mushi-zushi (steamed sushi). Steam the cold sushi rice topped with the chicken-soboro. (It is also possible to micro-wave instead of steaming.) When steamed, garnish with the mitsuba and ginger.

KOBASHIRA CHIRASHI

Ingredients (4 servings): 4 cups sushi rice (pp. 2-3, ½ of 4 cups rice), 5⅖ oz (160 g) kobashira (adductor in a round clam), (A) 《4 Tbsp vinegar, 2 Tbsp sugar, ½ tsp salt》, 3½ oz (100 g) lotus root, (B) 《⅓ cup vinegar, 2 Tbsp sugar, ¼ tsp salt》, 1-2 Tbsp white sesame, 12 leaves of kinome (Japanese pepper)

Method: 1. Prepare the sushi rice (pp. 2-3).
2. Rinse the kobashira in salted water. Drain and combine with well-mixed (A).
3. Peel the lotus root. Cut in half lengthwise and then cut into thin slices. Put into vinegared water for some time to get rid of the harshness. Boil quickly in hot water with a little vinegar added. Remove to a bamboo colander immediately when the color changed and drain. Marinate in the mixture (B).
4. Mix the white sesame evenly with the sushi rice. Place in a bowl. Top with the well-drained kobashira and lotus root. Garnish with the kinome and serve.

A VARIATION OF TEKKA CHIRASHI

Ingredients (4 servings): 4 cups sushi rice (pp. 2-3, ½ of 4 cups rice), 7 oz (200 g) tuna, 1 Tbsp shoyu, 4 Tbsp shirasuboshi (dried young sardines), 2⅖ oz (80 g) takuan (pickled radish), 1 clove ginger, 1 Tbsp white sesame

Method: 1. Prepare the sushi rice (pp. 2-3).

2. Slice the tuna and cut into bite-sized pieces. Sprinkle the shoyu over.

3. Pour boiled water over the shirasuboshi to get rid of fishy smell.

4. Cut the takuan into thin slices and then into ⅛″ (5 mm) cubes. Mince the ginger.

5. Place the sushi rice in a small bowl and top with the tuna. Scatter the shirasuboshi, takuan and ginger over. Sprinkle with the white sesame.

CONGER EEL CHIRASHI

Ingredients (4 servings): 4 cups sushi rice (pp. 2-3, ½ of 4 cups rice), 10½ oz (300 g) broiled conger eel (store bought), 3 Tbsp mizanshou (Japanese pepper seeds boiled down in soy and sugar) (store bought)

Method: 1. Prepare the sushi rice (pp. 2-3).

2. Cut the conger eel into about 2″ (5 cm) pieces.

3. Mix the pepper seeds with the sushi rice, and place in a bowl. Top with the conger eel.

★If you like, you can pour tare over.

Tare: Boil 2 Tbsp mirin, add 2 Tbsp each of shoyu and sake and bring them to a boil and boil down until thick.

SALMON-ROE CHIRASHI

Ingredients (4 servings): 4 cups sushi rice (pp. 2-3, ½ of 4 cups rice), 4 Tbsp salmon roe, 10 leaves aojiso (green perilla), 1 oz (30 g) kaiware (white radish sprouts) or watercress, wasabi (Japanese horseradish)

Method: 1. Prepare the sushi rice (pp. 2-3).

2. Roll the aojiso (green perilla) together and then cut into thin pieces from the end. Put in water for some time to get rid of the harshness.

3. Cut the kaiware into 1½″ (4 cm) lengths.

4. Place the sushi rice in a bowl. Scatter the drained aojiso over. Top with the salmon roe and garnish with the kaiware. Put wasabi on and serve.

SUSHI PACKED LUNCH

For busy morning, make maze-zushi by mixing sushi rice with ingredients as an easy way of making box lunch. Sushi rice can be made by mixing usual rice with vinegar mixture (p. 2).

Use well-drained plants.
BOX LUNCH OF WILD PLANTS

Ingredients (2 servings): 4 cups sushi rice (pp. 2-3, ½ of 4 cups rice), 3½ oz (100 g) boiled wild plants mix (store bought), 1¾ oz (50 g) boiled bamboo shoot, ½ fuki (butterbur), (A)《½ cup dashi stock, 1 Tbsp mirin, 1 Tbsp light shoyu》, 2 chicken breasts, (B)《2 tsp each of mirin, sake and shoyu》, 1 tsp salad oil, ¼ cod roe, 4 snow peas

Method: 1. Prepare the sushi rice (pp. 2-3).
2. Wash the wild plants and drain. Slice the bamboo shoot. Rub the butterbur with salt. Boil quickly in water and then put into cold water. Skin and cut into diagonal slices.
3. Put (A) and (2) in a pan and cook for some time until the ingredients are seasoned. Remove to a bamboo colander and drain.
4. Heat salad oil in a frying pan and brown both sides of the chicken breasts. Add (B) and then cut into pieces.
5. Bake the cod roe and cut into round slices. Boil the snow peas in salted water.
6. Mix the wild plants (3) with the sushi rice and pack into a box. Top with (4) and (5).

Just sprinkle over and mix.
GOSHIKI MAZE-ZUSHI BOX LUNCH

Ingredients (2 servings): 4 cups sushi rice (pp. 2-3, ½ of 4 cups rice), 1 fillet salted salmon, 1¾ oz (50 g) takuan (yellow pickled daikon), 3 Tbsp white sesame, 1 Tbsp yukari (minced salted shiso leaves), 5 aojiso (green shiso leaves), ½ squid, (A)《1 Tbsp each of mirin, sake and shoyu》, 4 Vienna sausages, 6 sprigs shungiku (garland chrysanthemums), 3 chrysanthemum flowers, 1 pack enokidake (velvet shank mushrooms), (B)《2 Tbsp each of vinegar and dashi stock, 2 tsp each of shoyu and sugar, dash salt》

Method: 1. Bake the salmon and flake. Combine the flaked salmon, minced takuan, white sesame and yukari and mix with the sushi rice. Pack all in a box and scatter over julienne aojiso.
2. Make incisions on the squid and grill. Boil down (A) and coat the squid with it. Sauté the sausages.
3. Boil the shungiku. Drop a bit of shoyu on it and cut into 1⅕" (3 cm) lengths. Boil chrysanthemum flowers and enokidake quickly. Combine with the shungiku and dress with (B). Pack in a box together with (2).

Enjoy a big bite.

MEHARI-ZUSHI BOX LUNCH

Ingredients (2 servings):
6 cups sushi rice (pp. 2-3,
3 cups rice), 4 takanazuke (pickled mustard leaves), 3
Tbsp white sesame, a bit of red pickled ginger, 4
slices kamaboko (boiled fish paste), 1 satsuma-age
(deep-fried fish-paste ball), (A) 《½ cup dashi stock, 1
tsp sugar, 2 tsp shoyu》, kogayaki (p. 54)

Method: 1. Prepare the sushi rice (pp. 2-3).
2. Separate the leaves and stalks of the takana.
Spread the leaves and cut in half. Chop the stalks
into fine pieces.

3. Mix the stalks and white sesame with the
sushi rice. Make four rice balls and wrap in the
leaves. Top with the red pickled ginger.
4. Cut the kamaboko into fan-shape slices. Cut the
satsuma-age into bite-sized pieces. Cook both in (A)
for a short time.
5. Pack (3), (4) and kogayaki into a box.
★The name "mehari (wide-opened eyes)" is said to
come from the fact: the size of the rice ball is so big
that those who look at it open their eyes wide or they
open their eyes wide when eating it. It was originated
by a woodcutter.

Goshiki (five-color) maze-zushi uses only five
kinds of ingredients. Other suitable ingredients
are cod roe, dried young sardines, dried
bonito shavings, poached eggs and toasted
nori.

TEMAKI-ZUSHI PARTY

How about serving temaki-zushi (hand-rolled sushi) to a party of close friends? It is a good chance to show your ideas.

This new sushi style is distinguished from ordinary rolled sushi in that the people who are going to eat it prepare it themselves. The sushi rice already mixed with filling ingredients is wrapped in other additional ingredients such as nori, lettuce, egg sheet and so on. It is luxurious sushi. Each participant can bring his or her own ingredients. In that case plain ingredients would be better.

Ingredients (5 servings):
● sushi rice 7½ cups (1½ cups per person) (pp. 2-3)
● **Mixing ingredients:** [A] 1 egg
[B] 4 Tbsp chirimenjako (dried young sardines), 3 Tbsp ground white sesame
[C] ½ cod roe, 5 aojiso (green perilla)
[D] 1⅖ oz (40 g) boiled bamboo shoot, kinome (young leaves of Japanese pepper)
[E] 1 oz (30 g) lotus root, 2 chrysanthemum flowers, 4 Tbsp salmon roe
● **Fillings:** 3½ oz (100 g) each of tuna, squid and herring roe, 1 broiled conger eel, 2⅘ oz (80 g) vinegared mackerel, 5 prawns, 2⅘ oz (80 g) roast beef
● **Wrappers:** 10 leaves each of leaf and iceberg lettuce, 5 sheets each of toasted nori and thin omelet (cut into a manageable size)

Method: 1. Mix 2 Tbsp sugar and dash salt with egg[A] and make scrambled egg (p. 12). Mix with the sushi rice.
2. Pour boiled water over the chirimenjako [B] and drain. Add the white sesame and mix with the sushi rice.
3. Wrap the cod roe [C] in plastic wrapper and cook in a microwave oven for about 1 minute. Strain it into powder. Cut the aojiso into thin strips. Mix the cod roe and aojiso with the sushi rice.
4. Slice the bamboo shoot [D] and cook in 2 tsp each of light shoyu and mirin. Mix with the sushi rice and garnish with the kinome.
5. Cut the lotus root [E] into fan-shape slices. Loosen the chrysathemum flowers. Boil both in vinegared water quickly. Marinate them in sweetened vinegar (2 Tbsp vinegar, 1 Tbsp sugar, ⅕ tsp salt) and drain. Mix with the sushi rice and scatter the salmon roe over.
6. Cut each filling into bite-sized pieces. Boil the prawn (p. 9) and cut open. Season the herring roe with a bit of mirin and light shoyu and tear with hands.
7. Wrap (1) ~ (6) in the wrappers as you like and serve yourselves.

C

D

MAKI-ZUSHI
(Rolled Sushi)

Preparing maki-zushi requires concentration. At first the result will be poor, but once you get the knack of it, you will soon become skillful.

Surprisingly simple. Practice makes perfect.

FUTOMAKI-ZUSHI (Thick Sushi Rolls)

Ingredients (2 rolls): 6 cups sushi rice (pp. 2-3, 3 cups rice), 6 dried shiitake mushrooms (p. 6), ⅔ oz (20 g) kampyo (dried gourd shavings) (p. 7), ¼ carrot, (A)《¾ cup dashi stock, 2 tsp sugar, dash salt, 1 tsp mirin》, 2 fillets white-flesh fish, (B)《1 Tbsp sake, 2 Tbsp sugar, ⅕ tsp salt, a bit of red food coloring or umezu (plum vinegar)》, thick omelet (p. 10), 4 springs spinach, 2 sheets toasted nori, amazu-zuke of chrysanthemum flowers (p. 64)

FILLINGS

Method: 1. Prepare the sushi rice (pp. 2-3).

2. Cook the shiitake in the same way as shown on page 6. Discard the stems and cut into ⅜" (1 cm) widths.

3. Cook the kampyo in the same way as shown on page 7.

4. Cut the carrot into ⅜" (1 cm) square sticks. Boil in (A) until soft.

5. Make denbu with the white-flesh fish as shown below.

6. Cook the thick omelet in the same way as shown on page 10. Cut into ¾" (2 cm) square sticks.

7. Boil the spinach. Arrange the leaves and stalks, piling alternately. Drop a bit of shoyu on top and wring.

8. See page 26 for wrapping and rolling. Wet the knife with a dish towel moistened with tezu (p. 26). Cut one roll into 8 parts. Arrange on the aspidistra leaf placed in the container. Garnish with the squeezed amazu-zuke of chrysanthemum flowers.

DENBU

| ① Remove bones and skin from the fish. Break the flesh over a low heat. | ② Stir-fry. When the flesh comes apart add (B). | ③ Continue frying taking care not to burn. Stir until soft. |

See page 26 for rolling
and pages 60-63 for the side dish and soup.

HOW TO MAKE THICK SUSHI ROLLS

Prepare tezu (mixture of the same quantity of vinegar and water) for wetting hands and subukin (dish towel moistened with tezu). Always keep your hands clean. Place the nori with the glossy side under with the shorter side at the top.

1

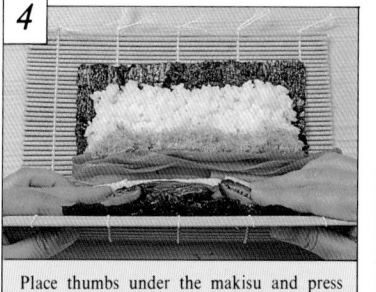

Lay a sheet of nori on the makisu (bamboo mat) and put half of the sushi rice on it.

2

Spread the rice, leaving a ¾" (2 cm) space on top and bottom. Make 6 grooves at intervals of ½" (1.5 cm) in the center.

3

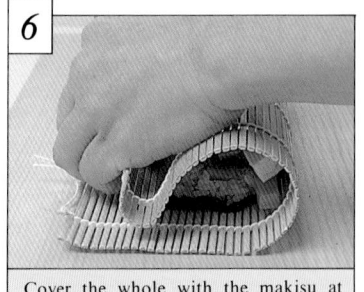

Place half of the 6 kinds of fillings each in its own groove with color in mind.

4

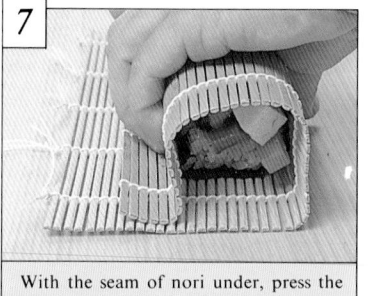

Place thumbs under the makisu and press the fillings with the fingers and lift.

5

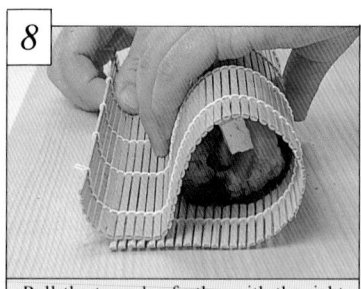

Holding the filling, bring the edge of the makisu toward the farthest side.

6

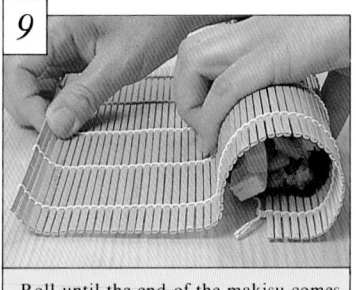

Cover the whole with the makisu at one stroke so that both edges meet.

7

With the seam of nori under, press the whole and adjust the shape with hands.

8

Pull the top edge further with the right hand, drawing the whole tightly toward you with the left hand.

9

Roll until the end of the makisu comes under and then remove the makisu.

10

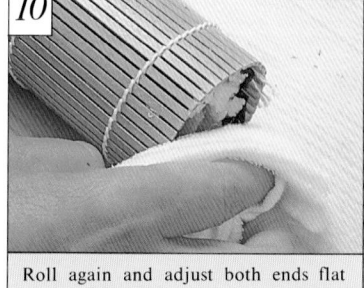

Roll again and adjust both ends flat with tightly squeezed subukin.

11

Completed nicely. Roll the other one in the same way.

12

Let it stand for some time and cut into 8 parts.

*Wipe the knife with subukin after every cutting.

More simple than thick sushi roll. Good for beginners.

HOSOMAKI-ZUSHI (Thin Sushi Rolls)

FILLINGS

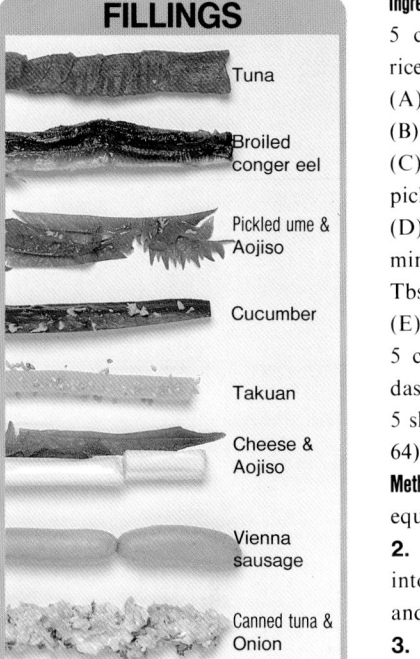

- Tuna
- Broiled conger eel
- Pickled ume & Aojiso
- Cucumber
- Takuan
- Cheese & Aojiso
- Vienna sausage
- Canned tuna & Onion
- Natto & Chives

Ingredients (5 kinds × 2 rolls):

5 cups sushi rice (pp. 2-3, 2½ cups rice)

(A) 1¾ oz (50 g) tuna, dash wasabi

(B) ⅓ cucumber, dash wasabi

(C) 1¾ oz (50 g) takuan (yellow pickled daikon), 1 tsp white sesame

(D) 1 small can of tuna, 1 Tbsp minced onion, 2 tsp minced parsley, 1 Tbsp mayonnaise, dash salt and pepper

(E) 1 pack natto (fermented soybeans), 5 chives cut into pieces, 1 tsp shoyu, dash mustard

5 sheets toasted nori, amazu-shouga (p. 64)

Method: 1. Divide the sushi rice into 10 equal parts.

2. Cut tuna, cucumber and takuan into ⅜″ (1 cm) square sticks. Mix (D) and (E) respectively.

3. Spread ½ sheet of nori on a makisu (bamboo mat) with glossy side under. Roll (A) ~ (E) 2 cylinders each and cut in bite-size as shown in the photo.

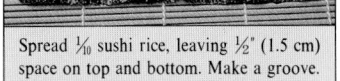

① Spread ¹⁄₁₀ sushi rice, leaving ½″ (1.5 cm) space on top and bottom. Make a groove.

② Spread wasabi lightly on the groove and put tuna pieces on it.

③ Bring both edges of the sushi rice together.

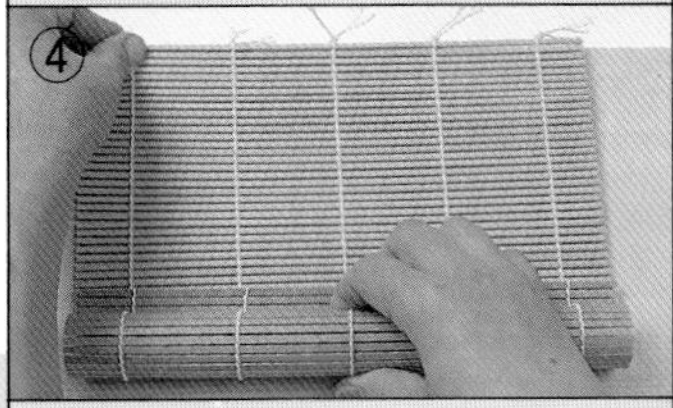

④ Roll and bring the whole toward you and press tightly.

A variety of maki-zushi with the nori inside. Looks like a whirlpool at Naruto.

NARUTOMAKI-ZUSHI

Ingredients (3 kinds, each 1 roll): 9 cups sushi rice (pp. 2-3, 4 cups rice), 1 cucumber, 3½ oz (100g) takuan (yellow pickled daikon), some white sesame, aonori (green laver) and oboro-kombu (shredded kelp), 3 sheets of toasted nori, amazu-shouga (p. 64)

Method: 1. Prepare the sushi rice (pp. 2-3).

2. Cut cucumber and takuan each into ⅜″ (1 cm) square sticks.

3. Place the nori on a makisu (bamboo mat) with the glossy side under with the shorter side at the top. Roll as illustrated in the photos. Roll 3 kinds (3 rolls) and cut each into ¾″ (2 cm) thick pieces. Garnish with the amazu-shouga.

● **Dusted with white sesame:** Follow steps 1~12 in photos.

● **Dusted with aonori:** Follow steps 1~11 in photos, and then use aonori instead.

● **Rolled with oboro-kombu:** Follow steps 1~9 in photos. Remove the plastic wrap. Affix the oboro-kombu to the sushi rice and roll together. Cut into ¾″ (2 cm) thick pieces.

★This sushi is also called 'Tatsumaki-zushi (tornado sushi),' 'Sotomaki-zushi (outside-roll sushi),' and 'Uramaki-zushi (Reverse-roll sushi).' Since the sushi rice comes outside, you can dust with anything you like. That is the point. Try dusting with other ingredients such as various furikake (seasoned powder for sprinkling over rice) and minced aojiso (green perilla).

★If you use two makisu, the reversion is easier (photo 3). In this case, lay another makisu on the plastic wrap. You can reverse it easily and continue the roll with the reversed makisu.

1 Spread 2 cups sushi rice on the nori.

2 Cut plastic wrap a little larger than the makisu and cover the sushi rice.

3 Turn over in one stroke. Remove the makisu and lay it on top of the makisu.

4 Spread 1 cup sushi rice on the nori.

5 Make a ¾" (2 cm) groove in the sushi rice nearest you. Put ⅓ of the filling on.

6 Put thumbs behind the makisu, holding the fillings with the other fingers and lift.

7 Bring the edges together, leaving a ⅜" (1 cm) space and roll.

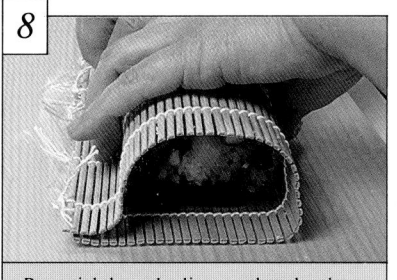

8 Press tightly and adjust so that the shape becomes square.

9 Adjust both ends flat and remove the makisu. Let it stand for some time.

10 Wet a knife with subukin (p.26) and cut together with wrap into ¾" (2 cm) thick pieces.

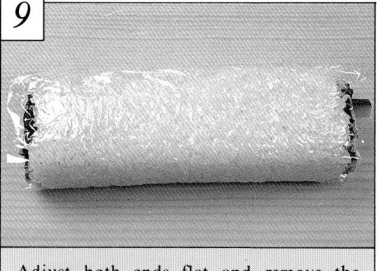

11 Remove the wrap carefully. The rice tends to stick to the fingers.

12 Spread the white sesame on a flat surface. Dust the sides evenly.

DECORATIVE MAKI-ZUSHI

FLOWERS

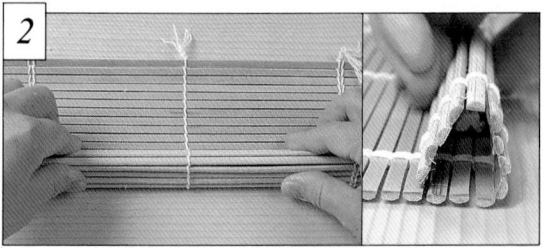

Ingredients (1 roll): 6 cups sushi rice (pp. 2-3, 3 cups rice), 1 egg, (A)《1 Tbsp sugar, dash salt》, ¼ carrot, (B)《½ cup dashi stock, 1 Tbsp sugar, ⅓ tsp salt, 1 tsp light shoyu》, 1 Tbsp minced pickled red turnip (store bought), 1 Tbsp minced cucumber pickled in shoyu (store bought), 1 Tbsp black sesame, 1 Tbsp aonori (green laver), 3½ sheets toasted nori

Method: 1. Prepare the sushi rice (pp. 2-3).

2. Mix (A) with the egg, and make scrambled egg (p. 12).

3. Mince the carrot and cook in (B).

4. Divide 2 cups sushi rice into 6 portions. Mix scrambled egg, carrot, pickled red turnip, pickled cucumber, sesame and aonori each with a portion of sushi rice.

5. Lay ⅓ sheet nori on a makisu (bamboo mat) with glossy side under. Spread the sushi rice mixed with carrot evenly, leaving ¾" (2 cm) space on the farthest side (photo 1). Roll, holding tightly and adjust the shape into a triangle (photo 2).

6. Roll the other 5 portions of sushi rice in the same way (photo 3).

7. Lay 1 sheet nori on a makisu. Add ½ sheet nori, joining ⅜" (1 cm) on top of each other. Glue together with mashed sushi rice. Spread 4 cups sushi rice, leaving ¾ " (2 cm) space on the farthest side (photo 4).

8. Assemble (6) into a cylinder. Place them in the center of the sushi rice (photo 5).

9. Holding the cylinder (photo 6), roll and adjust the shape tightly.

10. Let it stand for some time. Wet a knife with subukin (p. 26), and cut the whole into 8 parts.

WHIRLPOOL

Ingredients (1 roll): 6 cups sushi rice (pp. 2-3, 3 cups rice), 1 Tbsp minced pickled red turnip, 1 egg, (A)《1 Tbsp sugar, dash salt》, 3 Tbsp aonori (green laver), 3 Tbsp white sesame, 3⅓ sheets toasted nori

Method: 1. Prepare the sushi rice (pp. 2-3).

2. Mix (A) with the egg, and make scrambled egg (p. 12).

3. Divide the sushi rice into ⅓ cup, ⅔ cup, 1½ cups and 3½ cups. Mix ⅓ cup rice with red turnip, ⅔ cup rice with scrambled egg, and 1½ cups rice with aonori. (Reserve 3½ cups rice).

4. Lay ⅓ sheet nori on a makisu (bamboo mat) with glossy side under. Spread the sushi rice mixed with red turnip evenly, leaving ⅜" (1 cm) space on the farthest side. Roll, and adjust the shape into a cylinder.

5. Lay ½ sheet nori on a makisu, and spread the sushi rice mixed with scrambled egg evenly, leaving ⅜" (1 cm) space on the farthest side. Make a groove in the center and put (4) on (photo 1). Roll, holding the whole tightly, and adjust the shape into a square (photo 2).

6. Lay 1 sheet nori on a makisu. Spread the sushi rice mixed with aonori, leaving ¾" (2 cm) space on the

farthest side. Make a groove in the center and put (5) on (photo 3). Roll, holding the whole tightly, and adjust the shape into a square.

7. Lay 1 sheet nori on a makisu. Add ½ sheet nori, joining ⅜"(1 cm) on top of each other. Glue together with mashed sushi rice. Spread the plain sushi rice, leaving ¾"(2 cm) space on the farthest side. Sprinkle the white sesame over and put (6) on (photo 4). Roll, holding the whole tightly, and adjust the shape into a square.

8. Let it stand for some time. Cut the whole into 8 parts.

CARE AND HANDLING OF MAKISU

● Select a makisu made of slender strips of bamboo woven tightly with cotton string. After use, wash well with a brush and dry at an airy place. If it is not dried completely, it is likely to get moldy.

● The size varies depending on the use. An all-purpose one is a large mat, 12"(30 cm) by 12"(30 cm). Mats for thin rolls and hand rolls are also available on the market. It is also possible to make use of the mat for Japanese cakes.

● The surface of one side of the mat is smooth and the other side is rough. You can use either side you

like. In this book, the bamboo mat has been used with the smooth surface up when the shape of rolls requires a triangle or a square. This is because it is easier to adjust the angles.

INARI-ZUSHI
(Sushi Rice in Fried Tofu Bags)

The shape, size and fillings vary according to regions and families, which are proud of their own oinari-san (inari-zushi).

What is common to all is the use of well-seasoned abura-age (fried tofu).

Ingredients (12 pieces): 6 abura-age, (A)《1½ cups dashi stock or water, 3 Tbsp sugar, 4~5 Tbsp shoyu, 2 Tbsp each of sake and mirin》, 4~5 cups sushi rice (pp. 2-3, ½ of 4 cups rice), 2 Tbsp white sesame, 3 dried shiitake mushrooms, (B)《½ cup water in which shiitake was soaked, 1 Tbsp each of sugar, sake and shoyu, ½ Tbsp mirin》, ⅓ oz (10 g) kampyo (dried gourd shavings), (C)《1 cup dashi stock, 1 Tbsp each of sugar and shoyu, ½ Tbsp mirin》, ¼ carrot, (D)《½ cup dashi stock, 1 tsp sugar, ½ tsp mirin, dash salt》, amazu-shouga (sweet-sour pickled ginger) (p. 64)

Method: 1. Cook the abura-age as shown on page 33.
2. Prepare the sushi rice (pp. 2-3).
3. Cook the dried shiitake mushroom (p. 6) in (B), and kampyo (p. 7) in (C). Cut both into fine pieces. Mince the carrot and cook in (D).
4. Combine the white sesame with the sushi rice, and add drained (3) and mix well. Divide into 12 rice balls.
5. Complete by following steps 1~3 below. Garnish the amazu-shouga.

1

Squeeze the abura-age lightly and drain. Fill it with the sushi rice.

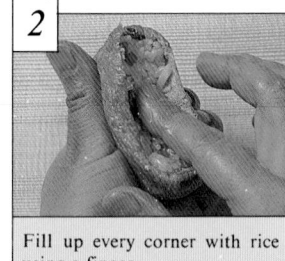

2

Fill up every corner with rice using a finger.

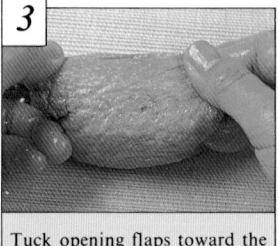

3

Tuck opening flaps toward the opposite side.

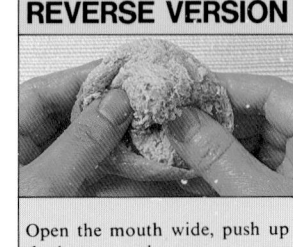

REVERSE VERSION

Open the mouth wide, push up the bottom and reverse.

ABURA-AGE (Fried Tofu)

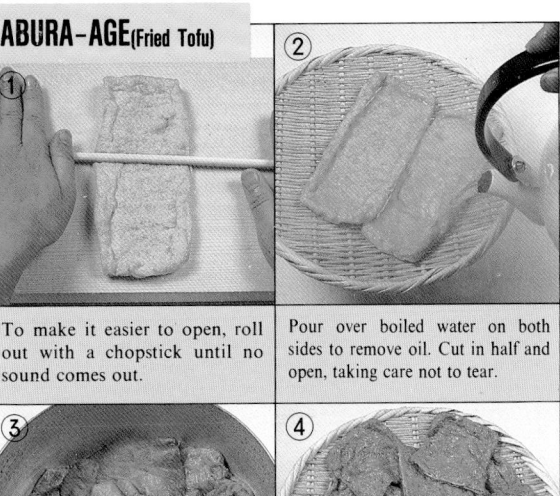

To make it easier to open, roll out with a chopstick until no sound comes out.

Pour over boiled water on both sides to remove oil. Cut in half and open, taking care not to tear.

Cook in (A) until almost all the liquid has evaporated. If possible, let them stand overnight.

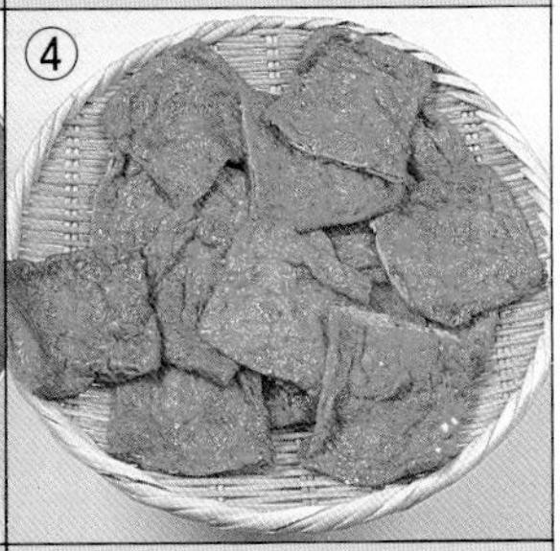

Spread on a bamboo colander, and leave them as they are until the liquid is strained off.

VARIOUS FILLINGS

● Presented here are examples of well-suited combinations of fillings, but you may combine any fillings you like.

● Don't spare time and effort to savor a delicious taste. Toast the sesame, pour boiled water over the chirimenjako, and so on.

● The fillings of san-shoku-inari (p. 34) and pocket-inari (p. 35) are not covered, so give attention to the combination of colors.

● If you mince the ingredients of chirashi-zushi (pp. 6-9), you can use them as the fillings of inari-zushi. Drain off the liquids well before mixing.

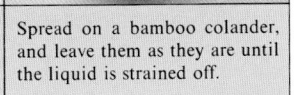

Chirimenjako
(dried young sardines)

Kinome   White sesame
(young leaves of Japanese pepper)

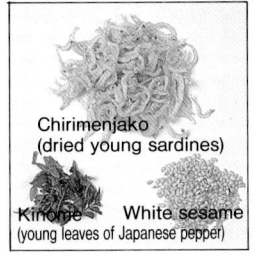

Poppy seeds

Cucumber

Kani-kamaboko
(boiled fish paste in the guise of crab)

Minced Fillings for Chirashi-zushi

Lotus root

Carrot   Dried shiitake mushrooms

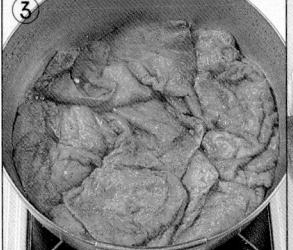

See pages 60-63 for kobachi and suimono.

VARIATIONS OF INARI-ZUSHI

TRIANGLE INARI

Ingredients (12 pieces) & method: 1. Pour boiled water over 6 square abura-age to remove oil. Cut each in half diagonally and open. Cook in the same way as on pages 32-33.

2. Mix any fillings you like with 4~5 cups sushi rice. Divide and press lightly making 12 rice balls.

3. Wring lightly and drain off liquid of abura-age. Reverse 6 abura-age and fill them with sushi-rice (2).

★Fill the sushi rice tightly in the bag reaching as far as the point of the triangle.

SANSHOKU INARI
(Three-colored Inari)

Ingredients (12 pieces) & method: 1. Pour boiled water over 6 square abura-age to remove oil. Cut each in half diagonally and open. Cook in the same way as on pages 32-33.

2. In a pan add 7 oz (200 g) ground chicken, 1 Tbsp sake, 2 Tbsp each of sugar and shoyu and stir-fry until the chicken is crumbled.

3. Mince ¼ carrot. Cook in ½ cup dashi stock, 1 tsp sugar, ½ tsp mirin and a dash salt.

4. Boil 16 field-pea pods in salted water and cut into fine pieces.

5. Mix 2 Tbsp white sesame with 4~5 cups sushi rice. Divide and press lightly making 12 rice balls. Insert in the abura-age (1).

6. Top with (2)~(4) using a spoon.

★You may add denbu (p. 24) or scrambled egg (p. 12).

CHAKIN INARI

Ingredients (12 pieces) & method: 1. Cook 6 abura-age in the same way as on pages 32-33.

2. Cook ⅔ oz (20g) kampyo (dried gourd shavings) as shown on page 7. Don't overcook or it will become too soft. Cut 12 pieces in 8" (20 cm) lengths.

3. Mix any fillings you like with the sushi rice and fill the abura-age tightly. Tie with the kampyo string.

★Reducing the quantity of sushi rice will make it easier to tie and adjust the shape.

POCKET INARI

Ingredients (12 pieces) & method: 1. Cook 6 abura-age in the same way as on pages 32-33.
2. Cut 1 cucumber and 4 kani-kamaboko (imitation crab made of boiled fish paste) into ⅛" (5 mm) cubes. Pour boiled water over 4 Tbsp young sardines.
3. Mix 2 Tbsp white sesame and (2) with 4~5 cups sushi rice.
4. Tuck in the mouth of abura-age and fill in (3).
★This is also called 'gunkan (warship) inari' since it looks like a ship. As the brim is tucked in, it is easy to fill in. In the case of ordinary inari-zushi, if you tuck about ⅓ of the mouth outward, you can easily fill it in.

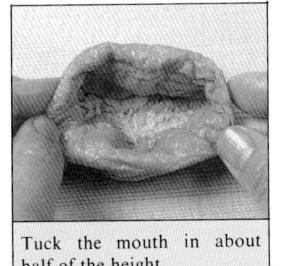

Tuck the mouth in about half of the height.

SHINODA-MAKI

Ingredients (12 pieces) & method: 1. Pour boiled water over 6 abura-age to remove oil. Cook in the same way as on pages 32-33. Cut off three sides and open.
2. Cook ⅔ oz (20 g) kampyo (dried gourd shavings) rather hard as shown on page 7.
3. Mix fillings as you like with 4~5 cups sushi rice. Divide into 6 parts. Spread on (1) lengthwise and roll up.
4. Tie two places with the kampyo and cut into two.

Cut off three sides and open carefully.

JUMBO INARI

Ingredients (8 pieces) & method: 1. Pour boiled water over 4 abura-age to remove oil. Cut in half and open. Cook in 1 cup dashi stock, 3 Tbsp each of sugar and shoyu, 2 Tbsp each of sake and mirin.
2. Cut ⅓ carrot into sticks. Add 5¼ oz (150 g) boiled mixture of edible wild plants. Cook all in 1 cup dashi stock, 2½ Tbsp shoyu and 2 tsp each of sake and mirin until tender.
3. Mix 2 Tbsp white sesame with 4~5 cups sushi rice. Add drained (2) and mix roughly. Divide into 8 parts and press lightly into rice balls.
4. Open the mouth of the abura-age and fill in (3). Shape so that the contents show.

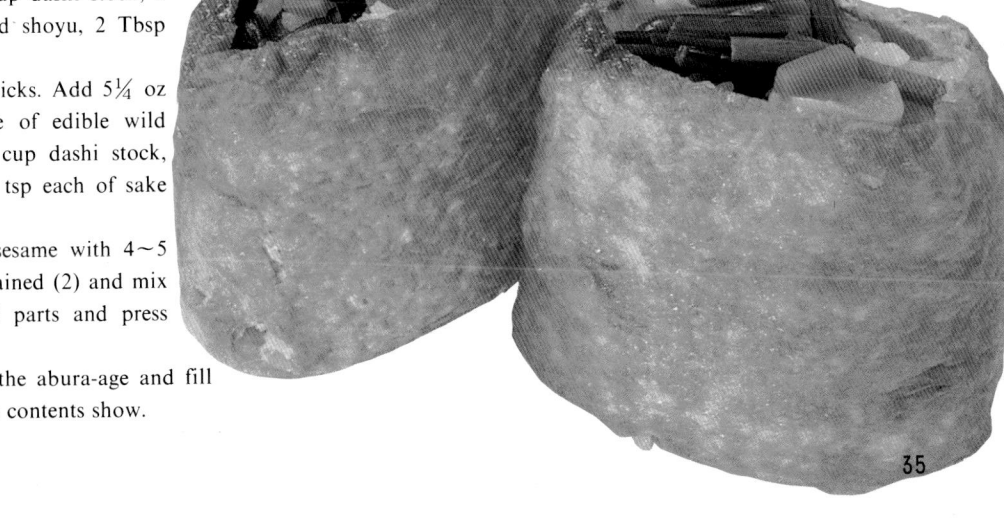

OSHI-ZUSHI & BOU-ZUSHI
(Pressed Sushi & Bar-shaped Sushi)

These are Kansai-style sushi which pile up the sushi rice and ingredients using a mold or makisu. When let to rest, they are well seasoned, so they are good for presents and parties. Even if the special mold is not available, you can make them. They are worth trying.

> When the mold is unavailable, use a rectangular pan or a lunch box.

OSHI-ZUSHI OF PRAWN

■ **Ingredients (for 7″ (18 cm) × 4½″ (12 cm) × 2″ (5 cm) mold)**
6 cups sushi rice (pp. 2-3, 3 cups rice), 7~8 prawns, (A) 《4 Tbsp vinegar, 2 Tbsp sugar, ¼ tsp salt》, 2 cucumbers, amazu-shouga (sweet-sour pickled ginger) (p. 64)
Method: 1. Prepare the sushi rice (pp. 2-3).
2. Boil prawn as shown on page 9 until bright red. Shell, remove the head and tail and open. Marinate in (A).
3. Cut 1 cucumber to the length of the mold and slice. Rub salt on another cucumber and cut into

8 decorative pieces.
4. Drain liquid off prawn and make oshi-zushi following the process, photos 1~6.
5. Take the plastic wrap off and cut into 8 pieces, wiping the knife occasionally with subukin (p. 26). Place on a plate and garnish with decorative cucumbers and amazu-shouga.

★When the lid (photo 5) is not available, cut cardboard or styrene foam to match the mold and use it instead.

1 Spread plastic wrap a little larger than the mold, which is large enough to contain prawn.

2 Arrange prawn alternately and spread half of sushi rice evenly over them.

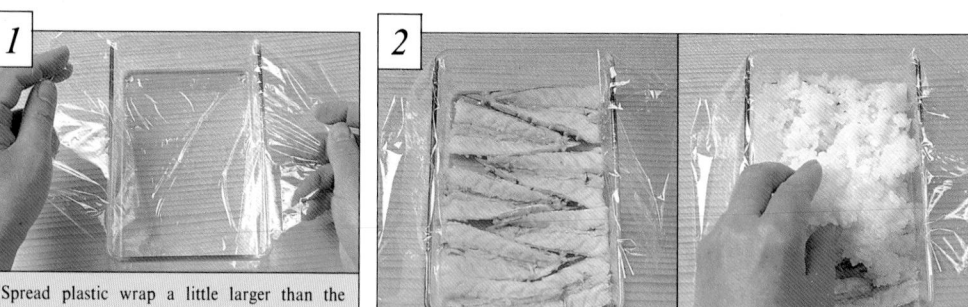

3 Arrange cucumber cuts compactly and spread the remaining sushi rice evenly over them.

4 Fold the plastic wrap and cover all tightly.

See pages 60~63 for kobachi and suimono.

5

Leave as they are for some time until well seasoned. As a weight, you can use a brick, books or cans.

Put on a lid (or substitute) and place a weight on it.

6

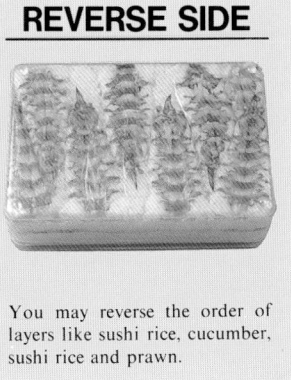

Remove the whole with the wrap and place on a board with the prawn side up.

REVERSE SIDE

You may reverse the order of layers like sushi rice, cucumber, sushi rice and prawn.

37

Girls will be delighted. Use a pan.

ICHIMATSU OSHI-ZUSHI

Ingredients (for 6″ (15 cm)×6″ (15 cm)×2″ (5 cm) mold): 6 cups sushi rice (pp. 2-3, 3 cups rice), ½ cup ebi-oboro (mashed shrimp) (store bought), 2 eggs, (A)《2 Tbsp sugar, ¼ tsp salt》, ½ carrot, (B)《⅔ cup dashi stock, 2 tsp sugar, ⅕ tsp salt, 1 tsp light shoyu》, 20 field-pea pods, aojiso (green perilla), umezu-shouga (ume-vinegar pickled ginger)

Method: 1. Prepare the sushi rice (pp. 2-3).

2. Break and beat the eggs in a pan. Add (A) and stir-fry to make scrambled eggs.

3. Mince the carrot and cook in (B) until tender. Drain off the liquid.

4. Boil the field-pea pods in salted water. Remove immediately into cold water and let cool. Drain off the water and mince.

5. Wet the mold and follow the steps in the photos. When filling the sushi rice, press it with hands each time, spreading evenly.

6. In advance, cut a cardboard to match the mold. Use it as a lid and place it over plastic wrap. Add a weight and allow it to stand for some time.

7. Take out of the mold. Wetting a knife with subukin (p. 26) cut into 4 parts. Put on the aojiso placed on a plate and garnish with the umezu-shouga.

1 Fill in ⅓ sushi rice, scatter field-pea pods over and put on ½ of remaining sushi rice.

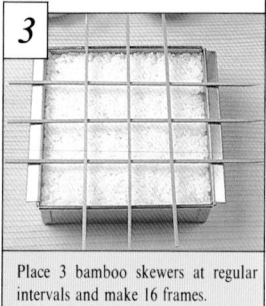

2 Add the carrot and spread remaining sushi rice.

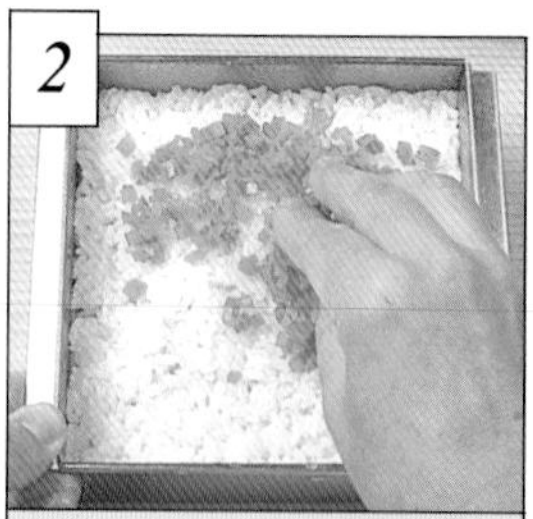

3 Place 3 bamboo skewers at regular intervals and make 16 frames.

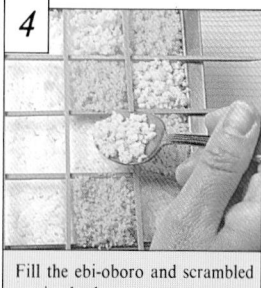

4 Fill the ebi-oboro and scrambled egg in check patterns.

5 Remove the skewers and cover with plastic wrap.

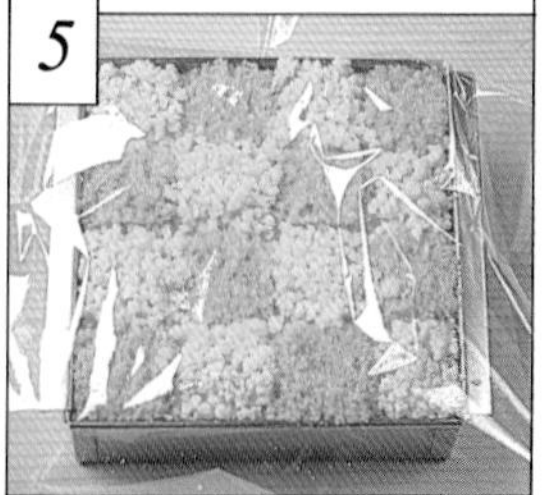

38

Mouth-watering sushi. Use a special mold.

OSHI-ZUSHI OF SALMON

■Ingredients (for 8 ⅜″ (21 cm) × 3″ (7.5 cm) × 2″ (5 cm) mold): 6 cups sushi rice (pp. 2 ~ 3, 3 cups rice), 3 Tbsp white sesame, 1 clove ginger (julienne), 14 oz (400 g) fresh salmon, ½ cup salt, (A)⟨½ cup vinegar, 3~4 Tbsp sugar, ⅔ tsp salt⟩, 6~8 kinome (young leaves of Japanese pepper), 2 myouga (Japanese ginger), (B)⟨2 Tbsp vinegar, 1 Tbsp sugar⟩

Method: 1. Prepare the sushi rice (pp. 2-3). Mix with the white sesame and ginger.

2. Place the salmon in a bamboo colander, sprinkle with plenty of salt and keep in the refrigerator for 2 hours. Or sprinkle with 2 tsp salt and wrap in a dehydrating sheet and keep in the refrigerator (p. 14). Rinse in water to remove the salt and marinate in (A) for about 30 minutes. Remove the skin and cut into slices.

3. Soak the wooden mold in water and wipe with subukin (p. 26). Follow the steps in the order of photos.

4. Serve on a plate and garnish with the sweet-sour pickled myouga (cut diagonally, put in vinegared water and marinated in (B)).

1 Fill the mold with the sushi rice. Spread and press evenly with hands, leaving no space in the corners.

2 Arrange salmon regularly and top with kinome. Cover with the lid.

3 Add a weight and leave it for some time. Holding the lid, ease the frame off.

4 Remove the lid. Wetting a knife with subukin (p.26) cut into bite-sized pieces.

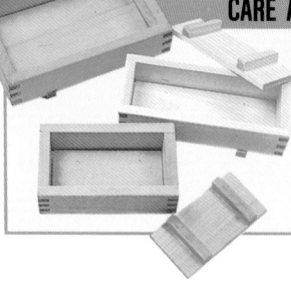

CARE AND HANDLING OF MOLD

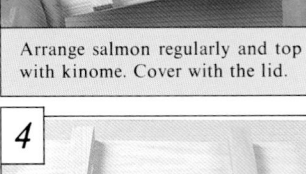

There are square and rectangle types of various sizes. Before using, soak in plenty of water so that it absorbs sufficient liquid. Next, wipe with a dry dish towel and then moisten with subukin (p. 26). After use, wash well and dry completely.

Use fresh mackerel. The best season is spring and autumn.

BOU-ZUSHI OF MACKEREL

Ingredients (2 bars): 6 cups sushi rice (pp. 2-3, 3 cups rice), 1 fresh mackerel, ½ cup salt, (A) 《½ cup vinegar, 3 Tbsp sugar, ⅔ tsp salt》, 1 sheet (4" (10 cm) × 18" (45 cm)) white kombu (kelp), (B)《½ cup vinegar, 3 Tbsp sugar, 2 tsp salt》, wasabi (Japanese horseradish), amazu-shouga (p. 64), sweet-sour pickled chrysanthemum flowers (p. 64)

Method: 1. Cut off the head of mackerel, gut and cut into three fillets. Remove bones and make shime-saba, following the steps in the photos (p. 41).

2. Prepare the sushi rice (pp. 2-3).

3. See page 41 for preparing the kombu.

4. Make the bou-zushi, following the steps in photos 1~11.

5. Allow it to stand for some time. Wipe a knife with subukin (p. 26) and cut into bite-sized pieces. Place on aspidistra leaves and garnish with the amazu-shouga and pickled chrysanthemum flowers.

★Fresh mackerel is very perishable, so it is important to make preparations for cooking immediately after buying.

★Choose fresh mackerel of which the underside shows a silvery sheen. The flesh in early spring and autumn is oily and the flavor is best. It should have clear eyes, bright coloring and be stiff.

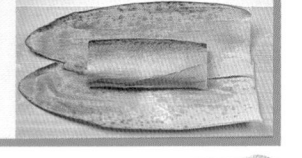

PRESERVATION

When you don't eat it immediately, or keep it for a present, wrap in bamboo sheaths and arrange in a pan with a weight put on for half a day to one day. The bamboo sheaths should be soaked in water in advance and wiped with vinegared water.

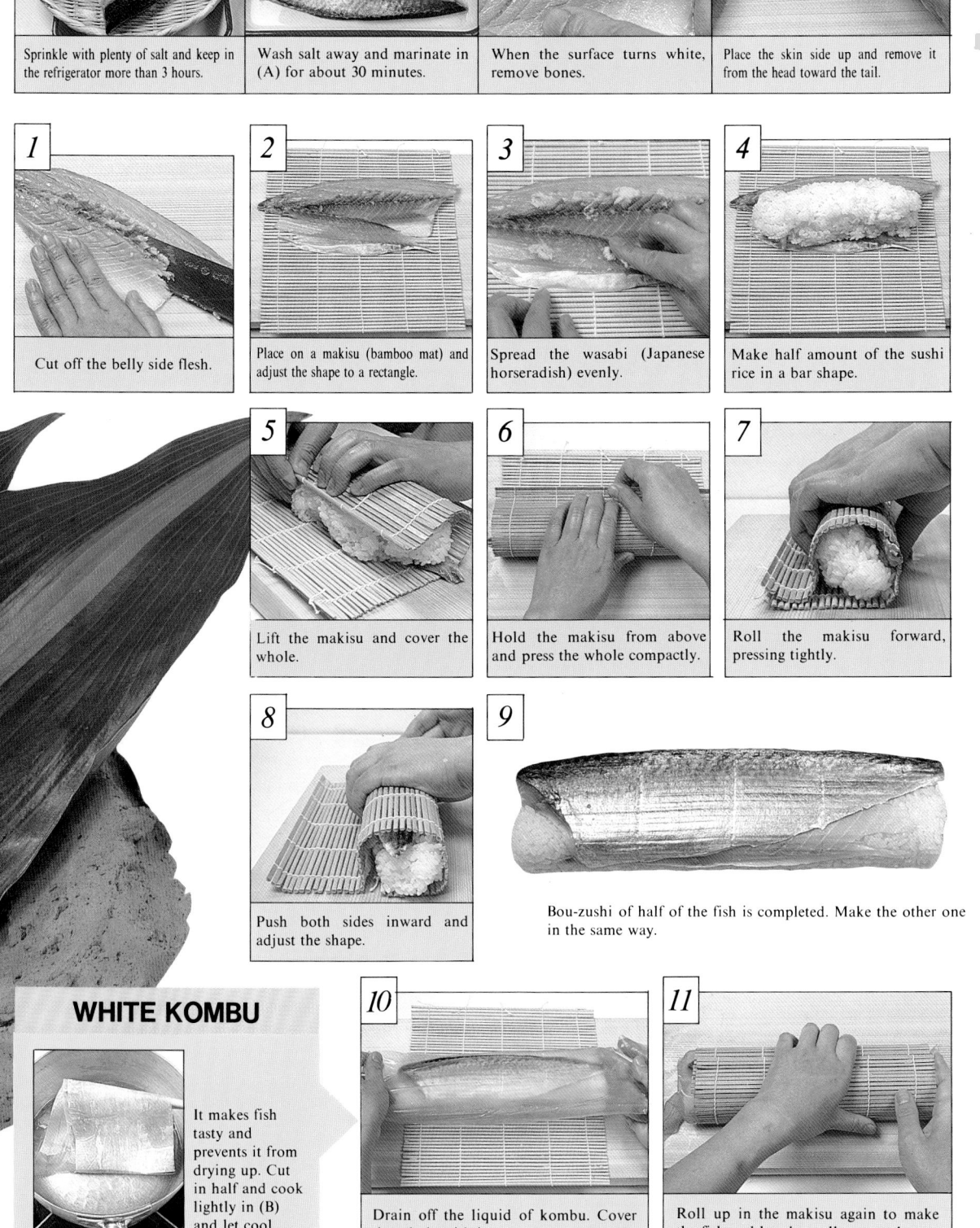

SHIME-SABA
(Vinegared Mackerel)

① Sprinkle with plenty of salt and keep in the refrigerator more than 3 hours.

② Wash salt away and marinate in (A) for about 30 minutes.

③ When the surface turns white, remove bones.

④ Place the skin side up and remove it from the head toward the tail.

1 Cut off the belly side flesh.

2 Place on a makisu (bamboo mat) and adjust the shape to a rectangle.

3 Spread the wasabi (Japanese horseradish) evenly.

4 Make half amount of the sushi rice in a bar shape.

5 Lift the makisu and cover the whole.

6 Hold the makisu from above and press the whole compactly.

7 Roll the makisu forward, pressing tightly.

8 Push both sides inward and adjust the shape.

9 Bou-zushi of half of the fish is completed. Make the other one in the same way.

WHITE KOMBU

It makes fish tasty and prevents it from drying up. Cut in half and cook lightly in (B) and let cool.

10 Drain off the liquid of kombu. Cover the whole with it.

11 Roll up in the makisu again to make the fish and kombu well seasoned.

41

Ginger-mixed sushi rice matches the taste of crab.

BOU-ZUSHI OF CRAB

Make when the saury are

BOU-ZUSHI

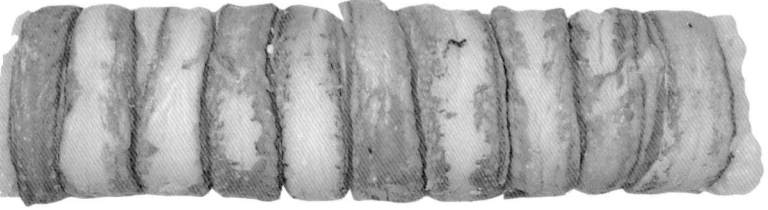

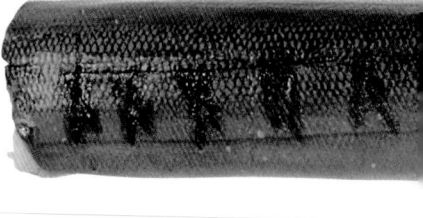

Ingredients (2 rolls): 5 cups sushi rice (pp. 2-3, 2½ cups rice), 1 clove ginger (julienne), legs of 1 crab (boiled), (A)《⅓ cup vinegar, 2 Tbsp sugar, ⅓ tsp salt》, amazu-shouga (p. 64)

Method: 1. Prepare the sushi rice (pp. 2-3). Mix with julienne ginger.

2. Remove cartilage from the legs of crab. Take care not to crush. Marinate in (A) for about 20 minutes. If the flesh is thick, slice it to a uniform size.

3. Place plastic wrap on a makisu (bamboo mat) and arrange half of the legs on it. Mold half of the sushi rice over it.

4. Lift the makisu together with the wrap and roll. When the legs come to the top, hold compactly, adjusting the shape and roll tightly with the wrap.

5. Make another roll in the same way, (3)~(4). Allow them to stand for some time.

6. Take off the wrap, and cut into bite-sized pieces with a knife, wetting with subukin (p. 26). Place on an aspidistra leaf arranged in a plate. Garnish with the amazu-shouga.

Spread plastic wrap on a makisu. Arrange legs with colored sides down.

Mold the sushi rice on the legs. Roll and adjust the shape.

TO CUT SAURY OPEN

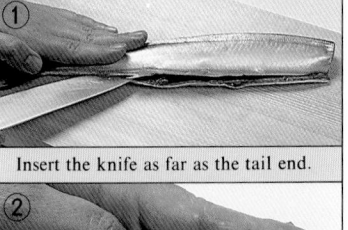

Insert the knife as far as the tail end.

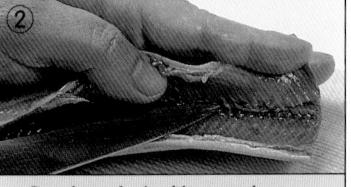

Cut along the backbone and open.

Slice off the bone and cut off at the tail end.

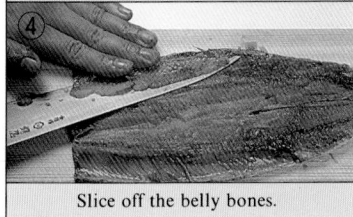

Slice off the belly bones.

OF SAURY

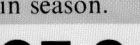

TAZUNA-ZUSHI
(Patterns of Japanese horse reins)

Ingredients (2 rolls): 5 cups sushi rice (pp. 2-3, 2½ cups rice), 3 Tbsp white sesame, 2 fresh sauries, ½ cup salt, (A)《½ cup vinegar, 3 Tbsp sugar, ⅔ tsp salt》, amazu-shouga (p. 64)

Method: 1. Cut off the head of saury and remove the entrails. Open the belly as shown in photos.

2. Sprinkle with plenty of salt and keep in the refrigerator overnight. Rinse off the salt and remove remaining bones. Marinate in (A) for about 20 minutes.

3. Prepare the sushi rice (pp. 2-3) and mix with the white sesame.

4. Place the saury on a makisu (bamboo mat) with the skin side down. Mold half of the sushi rice on it. Roll the whole so that the skin side comes top. Press tightly and adjust the shape. Make another roll in the same way.

5. Make criss-cross patterns on the skin and cut into bite-sized pieces. Garnish with the amazu-shouga.

Mold the sushi rice on the saury, roll and adjust the shape.

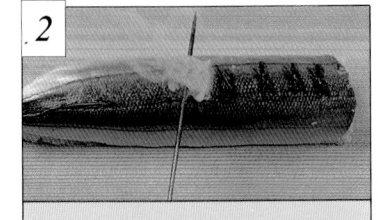

Make criss-cross patterns on the skin at even intervals with a heated metal skewer.

Ingredients (2 rolls): 5 cups sushi rice (pp. 2-3, 2½ cups rice), 2 halfbeaks, (A)《1 cup water, 2 tsp salt》, 4 prawns (p. 9), 1 cucumber, umezu-shouga (ume-vinegar pickled ginger)

Method: 1. Prepare the sushi rice (pp. 2-3).

2. Cut the halfbeak into 3 fillets. Slice off the belly bones and remove the backbone. Dip in (A) and remove the skin carefully from the tail.

3. Prepare prawn as on page 9.

4. Rub salt on the cucumber and cut into 2" (5 cm) lengths. Peel thinly all the way around. Cut diagonally into ¾" (2 cm) widths.

5. Spread plastic wrap on a makisu. Arrange half amount of (2)~(4). Mold half amount of sushi rice on them. Lift the makisu together with the wrap and roll the whole. When the fish and cucumber come to the top, press tightly and adjust the shape. Roll compactly in the wrap. Make another roll in the same way.

6. Cut together with the wrap. Peel off the wrap and serve. Garnish with the umezu-shouga.

Arrange the halfbeak, prawns, and cucumbers on the wrap with outside down.

Mold the sushi rice. Roll and adjust the shape.

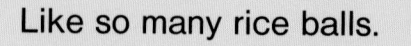

Like so many rice balls.

HORS D'OEUVRES SUSHI PARTY

Prepare 7~8 cups sushi rice for 4~5 servings. Make a variety of sushi, using cookie cutters or jelly molds.

[A] Salami: Shape the sushi rice with a jelly mold. Top with a folded salami slice. Tie with a boiled stalk of mitsuba (honewort).

[B] Smoked salmon: Make triangle or oval sushi rice balls. Top with the smoked salmon. Decorate with sliced cheeses cut into the shape of a star and kinome (young leaves of Japanese pepper). Squeeze out mayonnaise on them.

[C] Roast beef: Make sushi rice balls in the shape of a cylinder. Top with the roast beef. Decorate with slices of boiled okra and ham cut into the shape of heart.

[D] Cucumber, octopus & ark shell: Shape the sushi rice with a cutter. Place slices of cucumber. Top with thin slices of the octopus marinated in sweet-sour vinegar, ark shell and slices of small tomatoes. Tie the side of the rice ball with thin strips of toasted nori.

[E] Thin omelet & kani-kamaboko (imitation crab made of boiled fish paste): Shape the sushi rice with a cookie cutter. Top with the thin omelet cut with the same cutter. Add the kani-kamaboko, asparagus boiled and cut diagonally, salmon roes, and tie with boiled chives.

[F] Shiitake mushrooms boiled in sugar & sausage: Shape the sushi rice with a mold. Add shiitake boiled in sugar and cut into 8 parts radially. Sprinkle with poppy seeds and top with slices of radish, fried sausage. Decorate with asparagus boiled and cut into sticks and lemon slices.

★Arrange [A]~[F] colorfully on a tray. Garnish with parsley, olives and pickles.

44

Orthodox nigiri-zushi is difficult to make, but rice-ball style sushi is simple and easy. Devise new toppings and enjoy the variety.

MAKE USE OF CUTTERS AND MOLDS

Besides ordinary square and round rice balls, make lovely tiny rice balls with cutters and molds.

VARIATIONS OF TOPPINGS

Make mouthfuls of savory sushi like canapés. Avoid being unusual and choose the ingredients that match the sushi rice.

SEA URCHIN

Ingredients & method:
1. Make a triangle sushi rice ball. Add 3 cucumber slices and spread wasabi (Japanese horseradish).
2. Top with 1 Tbsp sea urchin and decorate with a lemon slice.

SALMON FLAKES

Ingredients & method:
1. Make a triangle sushi rice ball and put 2 lemon slices on it.
2. Top with 1 Tbsp salmon flakes (store bought) and decorate with kinome (young leaves of Japanese pepper).

SALMON ROE

Ingredients & method:
1. Make a triangle sushi rice ball and spread wasabi (Japanese horseradish).
2. Cut green parts of chives into $1\frac{1}{5}''$ (3 cm) lengths and put on the rice. Top with 1 Tbsp salmon roe.

HAM

Ingredients & method:
1. Make a triangle sushi rice ball and sprinkle with minced parsley.
2. Place square ham slices alternately and decorate with an okra slice boiled quickly.

PRAWN

Ingredients & method:
1. Make a square sushi rice ball.
2. Cook the prawn as directed on page 9, and open.
3. Sandwich thin sticks of cucumber and mayonnaise between the prawn and put on (1).

HERRING ROE

Ingredients & method:
1. Make a square sushi rice ball and spread wasabi (Japanese horseradish) on it.
2. Season desalted herring roe with a dash mirin and light shoyu. Put it on (1). Decorate with quickly boiled barilla.

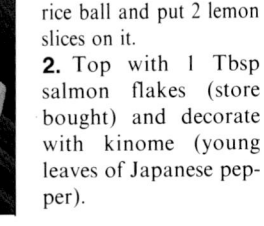

COD ROE

Ingredients & method:
1. Make a sushi rice ball.
2. Wrap the cod roe in plastic wrap and heat 1 minute in a hot microwave oven. Cut diagonally and put on (1).
3. Decorate with a small broccoli boiled in salt water.

PICKLES

Ingredients & method:
1. Make a square sushi rice ball. Place $1\frac{1}{2}''$ (4 cm) square slice of cheese on it.
2. Top with slices of pickles and decorate with red, green and yellow sweet peppers each cut into a diamond shape.

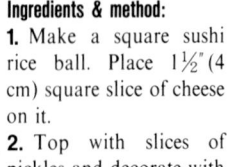

ARK SHELL

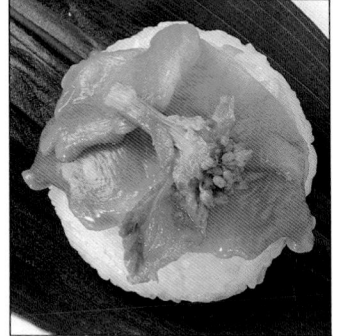

Ingredients & method:
1. Make a round sushi rice ball. Add a bit of wasabi (Japanese horse-radish).
2. Rinse the ark shell in salted water and place on (1).
3. Decorate with the top of a rape blossom boiled quickly in salted water and drained.

KAMABOKO

Ingredients & method:
1. Make a round sushi rice ball. Sprinkle with toasted black sesame.
2. Place on (1) 3 slices of kamaboko (steamed fish-paste cake) cut into a fan-shape.
3. Decorate with stalks of honewort boiled quickly and tied.

BOILED EGG

Ingredients & method:
1. Make a round sushi rice ball. Add a slice of soft-boiled egg.
2. Cut a green pepper in a ring and remove seeds. Pass a few daikon sprouts through it and put it on (1).

FERMENTED SOYBEANS

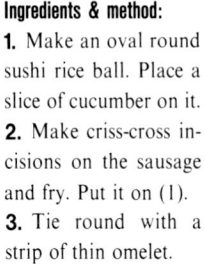

Ingredients & method:
1. Make a round sushi rice ball.
2. Add a bit of mustard and shoyu to fermented soybeans and mix well. Mount them on (1).
3. Decorate with chopped chives.

CANNED OIL-PACKED SARDINE

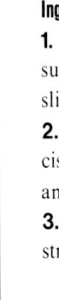

Ingredients & method:
1. Make an oval round sushi rice ball. Put on a smallish lettuce leaf.
2. Place a drained sardine on (1), and decorate with julienne red pepper and an onion slice cut into a ring.

VIENNA SAUSAGE

Ingredients & method:
1. Make an oval round sushi rice ball. Place a slice of cucumber on it.
2. Make criss-cross incisions on the sausage and fry. Put it on (1).
3. Tie round with a strip of thin omelet.

MUSHROOMS

Ingredients & method:
1. Make an oval round sushi rice ball. Add wasabi (Japanese horse-radish) and place aojiso (green perilla) on it.
2. Boil velvet shanks and shimeji mushrooms quickly and drain well. Place them on (1) in a well-balanced fashion.

GREEN ASPARAGUS

Ingredients & method:
1. Make an oval round sushi rice ball. Wrap round with a thin omelet.
2. Boil the top of asparagus in salted water. Drain off water and cut in half lengthwise. Put on (1). Tie round with a strip of nori (dried laver).

Get together bringing home-made cake sushi.

BIRTHDAY PARTY

The best treat at a party is delightful atmosphere and having a lively chat. No matter how skillful or unskillful, everyone should bring his or her own best sushi to the party and talk proudly about the result. See pages 50-51 for how to make these sushi.

Mini-zushi

Decorated-cake-style sushi

Sandwich-zushi

Too cute to eat.

MINI-ZUSHI

Ingredients & method: [A] Cherry tomato: Make a small square sushi rice ball. Top with a slice of cherry tomato, and decorate with corn and a green pea.

[B] Salami: Make a small triangle sushi rice ball. Wrap the salami around it and decorate with minced parsley.

[C] Smoked salmon: Mix minced parsley with sushi rice and make a small square rice ball. Place the smoked salmon and put mayonnaise on top. Wrap a kibinago(fish of herring family)around the tip of boiled asparagus and put in on the salmon.

[D] Roast beef: Make a small oval round sushi rice ball. Wrap the roast beef around it. Top with round slices of

boiled okra and put mayonnaise on top.

[E] Thin omelet & snow peas: Make a small round sushi rice ball. Wrap thin strips of omelet around it. Attach thin strips of a boiled snow peas to both sides of omelet. Decorate with salmon roe.

★Pack [A]～[E] in an empty chocolate box.

SMALL ROUND BALL

Wrap small amount of rice in plastic wrap and gather edges tightly.

SMALL SQUARE BALL

① Wrap rice in plastic wrap lengthwise. Pound lightly on a chopping board.

② Wet a knife with subukin (p. 26) and cut into pieces together with the wrap.

③ Adjust the shape into a square, pressing against the tip of the knife.

The taste is guaranteed.

SANDWICH-ZUSHI

Ingredients (for 4 servings): 6 cups sushi rice (pp. 2-3, 3 cups rice), 10 aojiso (green perilla), 10 small ume, 5 slices cheese, 3 slices ham, toasted nori, amazu-shouga (p. 64), lettuce

Method: 1. Prepare the sushi rice (pp. 2-3).

2. Roll up all the aojiso together and cut into fine pieces from the end. Mince the ume.

3. Mix half the amount of sushi rice with the aojiso. Add the ume to the remaining sushi rice and mix well.

4. Lay plastic wrap in a flat container and spread ume-mixed sushi rice. Arrange first cheese and then ham on it. Spread aojiso-mixed sushi rice over the ham. Fold the wrap down on both sides.

5. Cut a piece of cardboard to fit the container (or use another of the same size container). Place it as a lid. Put a weight (something like a brick) on it and allow it to stand for some time.

6. Cut into a triangle and tie with a strip of nori. Ar-

range on a leaf of lettuce and garnish with amazu-shouga.

★Make use of any container available such as molds on pages 36, 38 and a lunch box.

1 Lay plastic wrap in the container and spread ume-mixed rice.

2 Even out the sushi rice and arrange cheese and ham.

3 Cover with aojiso-mixed rice and even out the surface.

Congratulations!
DECORATED-CAKE-STYLE SUSHI

Ingredients (a diameter of 8" (20 cm)) : 12 cups sushi rice (pp. 2-3, 6 cups rice), 3 stalks of parsley, ½ carrot, (A)《½ cup dashi stock, 1 Tbsp each of sugar and light shoyu》, 3 eggs, (B)《2 Tbsp sugar, ⅕ tsp salt》, 16 prawns, 2 cucumbers, 40" (1m) kampyo (dried gourd shaving), (C) 《1 cup dashi stock, 1 Tbsp each of sugar and shoyu, ½ Tbsp mirin》

Method: 1. Prepare the sushi rice (pp. 2-3).

2. Mince the parsley. Mince the carrot and cook in (A) until tender.

3. Mix ⅓ sushi rice with the parsley and ½ of the remaining sushi rice with the carrot.

4. Break eggs in a pan. Add (B) and make scrambled eggs as directed on page 12.

5. Boil the prawns as directed on page 9. Shell them with the tail intact and open. Pour the amazu over (p. 9).

6. Wet a cake mold and proceed as shown in the photos 1~6 below.

7. Cut a piece of cardboard to fit to the mold and place it on (6) as a lid. Put a weight on top and allow to stand for some time.

8. Cut the cucumber into 3 portions and then into thin slices. Cut one end into points.

9. Cook the kampyo as shown on page 7 so that it remains firm.

10. Take out the lid and turn the whole over. Attach cucumber slices around it and tie with the kampyo.

★This serves 8~12 people. Press the sushi rice compactly so as not to collapse when cutting.

Arrange prawns radially with backs down and tails inwards.

Cover prawns with scrambled eggs.

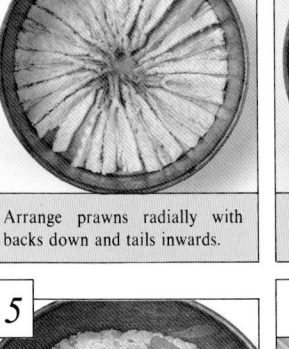

Spread plain sushi rice evenly.

Press with a lid and even out the whole.

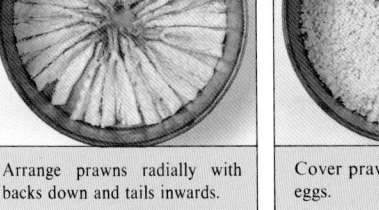

Spread carrot-mixed sushi rice and repeat (4).

Spread parsley-mixed sushi rice and repeat (4).

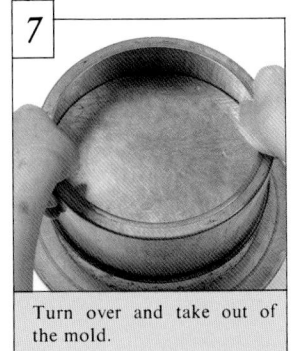

Turn over and take out of the mold.

FANCY SUSHI

Sushi varies from region to region. Here are some of the interesting sushi selected from all parts of the country. It will be fun to trace the root of each sushi.

The root is a fishing boat.
TEKONE-ZUSHI
(Sushi mixed with hands)

Ingredients (4-6 servings) : 8 cups sushi rice (pp. 2-3, 4 cups rice), 14 oz (400 g) lightly roasted or raw bonito, (A) 《6 Tbsp shoyu, 2 Tbsp mirin, 1 Tbsp sugar》, 1 tsp juice of ginger, 4 Tbsp white sesame, 3 pieces of ginger, 10 aojiso (green perilla)

Method: 1. Prepare the sushi rice (pp. 2-3).
2. Boil (A) in a small pan and allow it to stand to cool.
3. Cut the bonito into $\frac{1}{4}$″ (8 mm) thickness. Marinate in (2) with the ginger juice added for about 20 minutes.
4. Cut the ginger and aojiso into fine strips.
5. Mix the white sesame with the sushi rice. Add bonito slices together with the liquid and (4). Mix all with hands.
6. Serve in a small plate.

Photo for method (3)

★The feature of this sushi is that it is quick to prepare. It is said that fishermen originated this sushi with fresh-caught bonito. It has a dynamic taste. Instead of bonito, sardines or horse mackerels might be also used.

★Use plenty of ginger. Its flavor and pungent taste will rid the fishy smell of the sushi.

Local sushi in Nagano prefecture.

SASA-ZUSHI
(Bamboo leaf sushi)

Ingredients (24 pieces): 6 cups sushi rice (pp. 2-3, 3 cups rice), 2 Tbsp white sesame, ¼ ginger julienne, 2⅖ oz (80 g) raw sea bream, 8 shrimps, (A)《4 Tbsp vinegar, 2 Tbsp sugar, ¼ tsp salt》, 2 halfbeaks, (B)《1 cup water, 2 tsp salt》, wasabi (Japanese horseradish), metade (buds of water pepper), amazu-shouga (p. 64), 48 bamboo leaves

Method: 1. Prepare the sushi rice (pp. 2-3).

2. Cut the sea bream in slices.

3. Cook the shrimp according to page 9. Cut off the head and tail, shell and slit open. Cut in slices. Pour over vinegar mixture (A).

4. Cut the halfbeak into 3 fillets and slice. Pass through the salted water (B).

5. Combine ⅓ sushi rice and white sesame, and ½ of the remaining sushi rice and ginger. Mix well respectively. Divide into 8 portions respectively. Make the same division for the remaining plain sushi rice. Press in a square shape for each piece.

6. Wash bamboo leaves in water. Place 2 leaves crisscross. Add sesame-mixed rice and a dab of the wasabi (photo 1). Top with the sea bream (photo 2). Wrap with the leaves (photo 3) and put a rubber band around them. Make 8 pieces.

7. In the same way as in (6), make 8 pieces with ginger-mixed rice and halfbeaks, and the remaining 8 pieces with plain rice and shrimps.

8. Arrange (6) and (7) in a flat container and cover with another container (photo 4) and a weight. Let it stand for over 30 minutes so as to be well seasoned.

★If you leave it longer, it becomes more tasty, so it is good for a pleasure trip and presents. If you put the metade on the sea bream or amazu-shouga on the halfbeak when closing the leaves, you can savor a different pleasant taste.

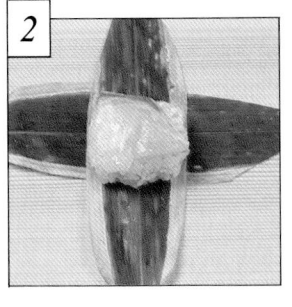

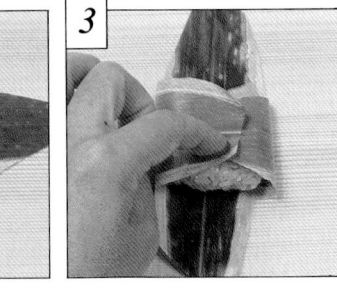

Deluxe sushi made by fermenting local sake of Kagoshima.

SAKE-ZUSHI

Ingredients (8 servings): sushi rice 《5 cups each of rice and water, 4″ (10 cm) kombu (kelp seaweed), 5 Tbsp sake, (A)(2½ cups local sake, 2 tsp salt)》

● **Mixing Ingredients:** 6 dried shiitake mushrooms (p. 6), 1¾ oz (50 g) takenoko (bamboo shoots) (p. 6), ⅔ oz (20 g) kampyo (dried gourd shavings) or dried daikon (Japanese radish) (p. 7), ⅓ ninjin (carrot) (p. 7), 2 satsuma-age (deep-fried fish-paste cake) (p. 7), ½ kamaboko (steamed fish-paste cake), 1 fuki (butterbur)

● **Decorating Ingredients:** kinshi-tamago (p. 8), 5¼ oz (150 g) renkon (lotus root), 5¼ oz (150 g) kibinago (round herring), 2 sayori (halfbeak), (B)《1 cup water, 2 tsp salt》, 3½ oz (100 g) tai (sea bream), ½ ika (squid), 8 ebi (prawn), 2⅖ oz (80 g) each of kobashira (adductor in a round clam) and aoyagi (round clam), (C) 《3 Tbsp vinegar , 1 Tbsp sugar, ⅓ tsp salt》, kogayaki (see below), kinome (young leaves of Japanese pepper) or mitsuba (honewort)

Method: 1. Prepare the sushi rice (photos 1-3).

2. See page 6 for the shiitake mushroom and bamboo shoots and see page 7 for the kampyo (or daikon), carrot and satsuma-age.

3. Cut the kamaboko in a fan-like shape. Rub the fuki lightly with salt and parboil. Transfer to cold water and peel the skin and cut into rolling wedges.

4. See page 8 for the kinshi-tamago and renkon.

KOGAYAKI

3 eggs (beaten)
⅙ cake tofu (crumbled)
⅞ oz (25 g) yam (grated)
1 fillet white meat of fish (chopped)
Condiments
  3 Tbsp sugar
  1 Tbsp mirin (or local sake)
  ¼ tsp salt
  1 tsp light shoyu

① Put all the ingredients through a blender and pour into a mold. Steam for about 40 minutes.

② Heat 1 tsp salad oil and fry to a brown color.

③ Turn over and fry in the same way. When cooled cut into strips.

1

Prepare the rice according to pp. 2-3. Pour heated (A) over with a ladle.

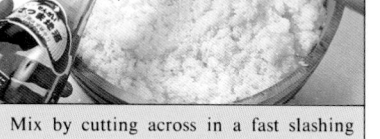

2

Mix by cutting across in a fast slashing motion. Add local sake as you like.

3

The sake will collect on the bottom, but it will be absorbed in over 6 hours.

MIXING INGREDIENTS

Dried daikon (or kampyo)

Ninjin

Takenoko

Fuki

Shiitake

Kamaboko

Satsuma-age

DECORATING INGREDIENTS

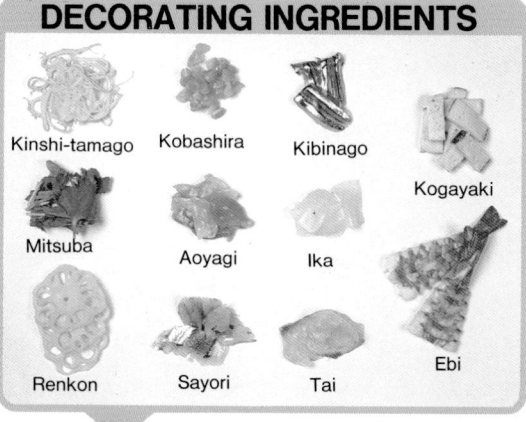

Kinshi-tamago   Kobashira   Kibinago

Kogayaki

Mitsuba   Aoyagi   Ika

Renkon   Sayori   Tai   Ebi

The kogayaki will also be used for mixing ingredients. It is not necessary to use all the ingredients. Make use of those available.

4

Scatter the mixing ingredients over and mix evenly.

5

Scatter the decorating ingredients over with the color in mind.

6

Cover with a larger plate and add a weight (ex. a brick). Let it stand for over 6 hours.

5. Cut the sayori into three fillets. Parboil in (B) and slice together with the tai and ika. Boil prawns as shown on page 9, and slit open. Rinse the kobashira and aoyagi in salted water and marinate in amazu (C).

6. Follow steps (4)~(6) when using a wooden tub. When a special tub for sake-zushi is available, prepare as follows: put ⅓ sushi rice mixed with ingredients in the tub. Then scatter over ⅓ ingredients for decoration. Repeat this procedure three times and make three layers. Cover with a lid and put on a weight.

7. Serve in a small plate.

★The local sake in Kagoshima is sweet like mirin. Adjust the quantity of sake as you like.

★Long ago, a lord gave a party under the cherry blossoms. After the party, the vassals collected the leftovers and poured sake over them and laid them aside. The next day they found that they turned out to be delicious. This is said to be the beginning of sake-zushi.

Just stuffing sushi rice. The origin of sushi.

IKA-ZUSHI (Squid sushi)

Ingredients (2 squids): 4~5 cups sushi rice (pp. 2-3, 2 cups rice), 2 fresh squids, (A)《½ cup vinegar, 3 Tbsp sugar, ⅔ tsp salt》, 3 Tbsp white sesame, 7 oz (200 g) edamame (young soybeans), 2 pieces shouga (ginger), 6 myouga (Japanese ginger), 10 aojiso (green perilla), 4 hojiso (head of aojiso), julienne aojiso

Method: 1. Prepare the sushi rice (pp. 2-3). The amount depends on the size of squids.

2. Remove the head from squid, cut off tentacles and clean. Wash in cold water. Prepare the body as shown below (photos 1-3). Chop tentacles and pour hot water over. You can pour hot water over the body if you like.

3. Boil soybeans in pods in salted water and shell to obtain 7 oz (200 g) beans. Mince the shouga, myouga and aojiso.

4. Mix the white sesame with the sushi rice evenly. Add squid tentacles and (3) and mix all lightly.

5. Stuff (4) in the body of squid and let it stand for some time.

6. Moisten a knife with subukin (p. 26) and cut the stuffed squid into ¾" (2 cm) wide pieces and serve in a plate. Garnish with hojiso and scatter aojiso over.

★The plain taste is a good accompaniment when drinking.

MIXING INGREDIENTS

Edamame   Myouga

Shouga   Aojiso

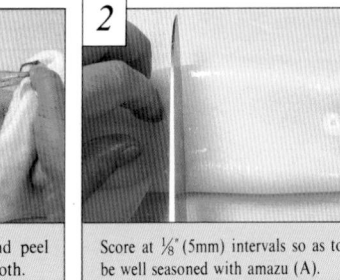

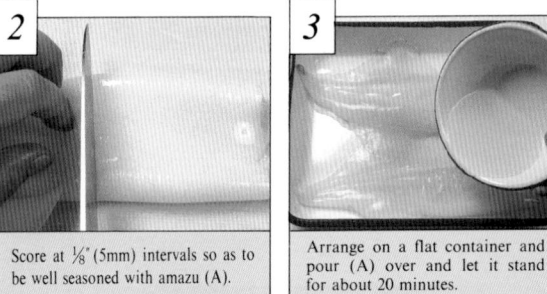

1 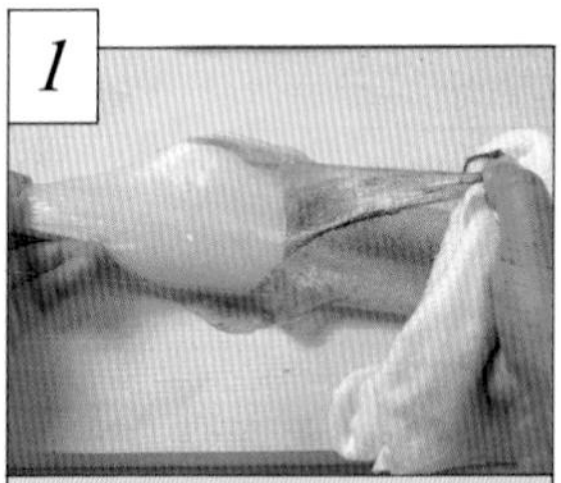 Remove the cartilage and peel the skin with a wet dish cloth.

2 Score at ⅛" (5mm) intervals so as to be well seasoned with amazu (A).

3 Arrange on a flat container and pour (A) over and let it stand for about 20 minutes.

4 Stuff the mixed sushi rice compactly and let it stand for some time.

Using plastic wrap. Take care not to squeeze too tightly.

TEMARI-ZUSHI
(Japanese Handball Sushi)

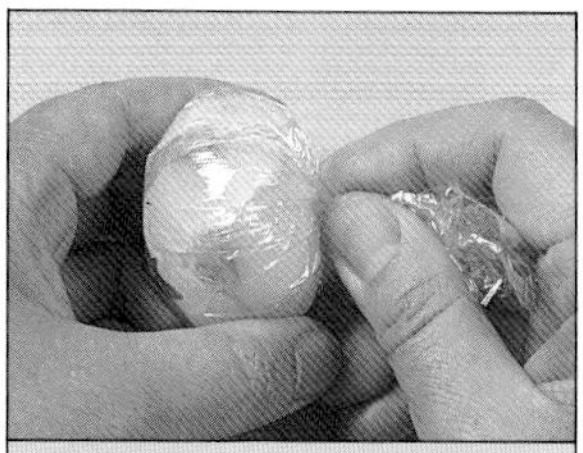

Put the ingredient and sushi rice on a piece of wrap in this order, make a round ball and twist the top.

Ingredients (7 kinds × 4 pieces): 6 cups sushi rice (pp. 2-3, 3 cups rice), $1\frac{2}{5}$ oz (40 g) each of fresh tuna and squid, 4 sasazuke of small sea bream (available at a store), 4 prawns, 4 fresh ark shells, 2 sheets each of thin omelet and toasted nori, 2 Tbsp ebi-oboro (crumbled shrimp)(available at a store), 8 kinome (young leaves of Japanese pepper), 1 Tbsp salmon roe, wasabi (Japanese horseradish), okra, amazu-shouga (p. 64)

Method: 1. Prepare the sushi rice (pp. 2-3).

2. Cut the tuna, squid and sea bream into slices. Boil prawns according to page 9. Slit open and slice. Rinse the ark shell in salted water and drain.

3. Spread plastic wrap and put $\frac{1}{4}$ tuna on it. Make a round ball of sushi rice, about the size of a ping-pong ball, and put it on the tuna. Gather each corner of the wrap to meet on the top and twist together. Be careful not to press too hard. Shape it like a hand-ball. Make another three balls in the same way.

4. In the same way as (3), make four rice balls each of the squid, sea bream, prawn and ark shell. Put kinome and wasabi under the squid and wasabi under other ingredients.

5. Cut the thin omelet and nori into four portions. (If the omelet is round, cut the edge and make it square.)

6. Place the thin omelet on the nori. Make a crisscross cut in the center and put on a wrap. Spread $\frac{1}{8}$ ebi-oboro in the center and put a rice ball on it. Bring up the sides of wrap and twist. Make another three balls. Reverse the order of omelet and nori and make another four rice balls in the same way. Widen the crisscross cuts when serving, and the sushi will look attractive.

7. Arrange (3)~(6) on a plate, and put wasabi on tuna, salmon roe on sea bream, and kinome on prawn. Garnish with okra boiled colorfully and amazu-shouga.

★If you twist the wrap too tightly, it will harden the sushi rice and spoil the taste, so use moderate force.

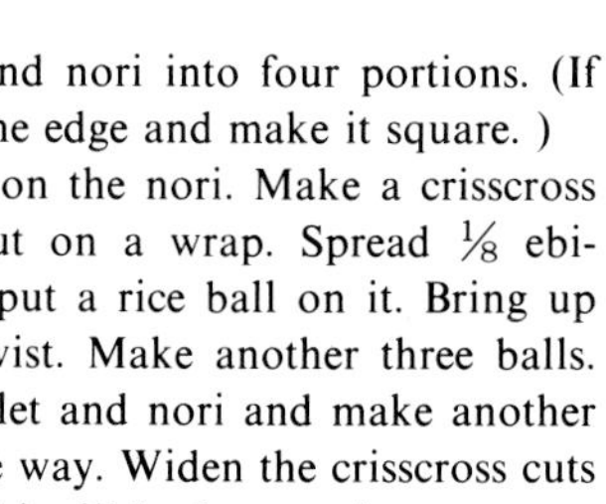

Widen the cuts a little so that the inside becomes visible.

VARIATIONS OF THIN OMELET SUSHI

Each quantity of the thin omelet, sushi rice and ingredients are the same for making 8 pieces.

8 sheets of thin omelet

Mixture
- 3-4 eggs
- 1 tsp sugar
- ¼ tsp salt
- 1 Tbsp cornstarch (water mixture)

Salad oil
Method: See page 8 for kinshi-tamago. For Hina-Zushi, cook 4 thin omelets, using ½ quantity of the above mixture.

3 cups sushi rice
Method: Prepare the sushi rice with 1½ cup rice as directed on pages 2-3.

Fillings
- 2 Tbsp white sesame(toasted)
- 5 dried shiitake mushrooms

Stock:
- 1 cup water in which mushrooms were soaked
- 1½ Tbsp each of sugar and shoyu
- 1 Tbsp sake
- 1 Tbsp mirin

- 8 kinusaya(snow peas)
- ¼ carrot

Stock:
- ½ cup dashi stock
- 1 tsp sugar
- Dash salt
- 1 tsp mirin

Method: Cook the dried shiitake mushrooms according to p.6 and chop into small pieces. Parboil the kinusaya and mince. Mince the carrot and cook in the stock until tender.

FUKUSA-ZUSHI (Wrapping Cloth Sushi)

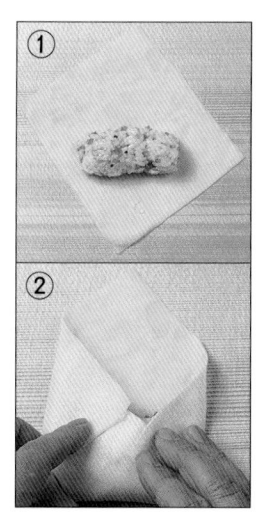

Method: 1. Mix the white sesame and the sushi rice. Combine drained filling ingredients and mix well. Divide into 8 portions and make 8 rice balls.
2. Cut the edges of omelet off and make a square sheet.
Spread it with one corner placed toward you (photo 1). Put (1) on and wrap as shown in photo 2.
3. Fix with a skewer and decorate with the kinome.

★Instead of using the skewer, you may tie it with parboiled mitsuba (honewort).

KINSHI-MAKI
(Rice Wrapped in Thin Omelet)

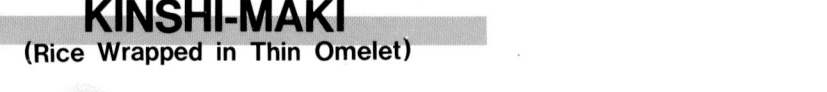

Method: 1. Mix the white sesame and the sushi rice. Combine drained filling ingredients and mix well. Divide into 8 portions and make 8 rice bars.
2. Cut the edges of omelet off and make a square sheet. Spread it with one corner placed toward you (photo 1). Adjust the shape and roll up. (If you use a makisu (bamboo mat), it will be easier.)
3. Place the end under and tie with parboiled mitsuba (honewort).

CHAKIN-ZUSHI (Gold-Wrapped Sushi)

Ingredients and method: 1. Cook ⅔ oz (20 g) kampyo (dried gourd shavings) so it remains firm according to page 7. Prepare 8 pieces, each 12″ (30 cm) long. Mince the remaining kampyo for filling.

2. Devein 4 shrimps and boil in water with salt and sake added. Cut a shrimp into 4 portions. Sprinkle 8 rape blossoms with salt and boil. Use only the tips. Mince the stalks for filling.

3. Mix the white sesame and the sushi rice evenly. Combine drained fillings (together with the kampyo and rape blossoms) and mix well. Divide into 8 portions and make 8 rice balls.

4. Spread the thin omelet and put (3) in the center. Bring the edges of the omelet up, gathering them on the top and tie with the kampyo. (Photo 1 and 2)

5. Open the edges of the omelet like petals and decorate with shrimps and rape blossoms.

completed

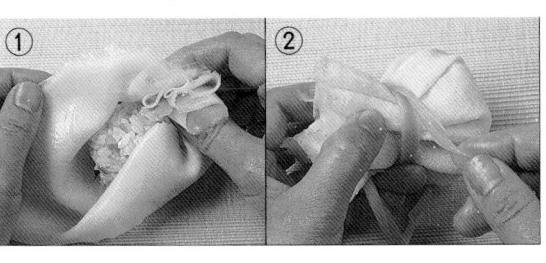

HINA-ZUSHI (Doll Sushi)

Ingredients (2 kinds × 4 pieces) and method: 1. Cook 4 sheets of thin omelet with ½ of the egg mixture on page 58. Cut in half.

2. Divide ¼ sushi rice into 8 portions. Fold each in plastic wrap and make a round ball to make a head.

3. Mix the remaining sushi rice and white sesame evenly. Combine drained fillings and mix well. Divide into 8 portions and make triangle rice balls.

Emperor　　　　　　　　　　　　　　Empress

4. Emperor: Spread the thin omelet with the curved side toward you and put (3) on. Cut aojiso (green perilla) in half and arrange above the rice ball. Fold the omelet like clothes and tuck in the bottom. Attach nori (hair), sesames (eyes) and carrot (mouth) to the face (2). Make headgear with cucumber and fix it to the head with a toothpick. Join the face and body with a bamboo skewer and insert a scepter of cucumber.

5. Empress: Make the body in the same way as the Emperor using carrot (softened with a sprinkle of salt) in place of aojiso. Make the hair (nori), eyes (nori) and mouth (carrot). Attach a crown of thin omelet and carrot to the head. Join the face and body with a bamboo skewer and insert a fan of cucumber.

★It requires a little time and effort to make this hina-zushi, but it is worth the challenge. Children will be delighted. You can make the face with a quail's egg, and just put on the headgear or crown. It will create a splendid atmosphere of hina dolls.

SIMPLE KOBACHI & SUIMONO

(Dishes in a Small Bowl and Soup)

CRAB & CUCUMBER IN SWEETENED VINEGAR (p. 25)

Ingredients (4 servings) and method: 1. Remove meat from 4 legs of boiled crab, remove cartilage and break up.
2. Cut 2 cucumbers into ring slices and rub with a pinch salt. Cut 1½" (4 cm) lotus root into fan-shape slices, and parboil in hot water with vinegar added.
3. Dress (1) and (2) with shouga-zu (2 Tbsp vinegar, 1½ Tbsp sugar, ⅓ tsp salt, 1 tsp ginger juice) and put on aojiso (green perilla) placed in a bowl. Top with ginger cut into julienne strips.

MOUNTAIN YAM, WHITE RADISH SPROUTS & UME PULP (p. 33)

Ingredients (4 servings) and method: 1. Cut 7 oz (200 g) mountain yam into sticks, ¼" (8 mm) square and 1½" (4 cm) long.
2. Remove the root of a pack of white radish sprouts and cut into 1½" (4 cm) lengths.
3. Dress (1) and (2) with bainiku-koromo (2 Tbsp ume pulp, 1 Tbsp dashi stock, ½ Tbsp sugar, ½ tsp shoyu).
4. Place in a bowl and sprinkle with nori torn to pieces.

GOBOU & ITO-KONNYAKU (p. 37)

Ingredients (4 servings) and method: 1. Cut ½ gobou (burdock root) into julienne strips. Rinse in water, changing water.
2. Drain off the hot water after boiling 5¼ oz (150 g) ito-konnyaku (strings of jelly-like food made from the starch of devil's tongue) to remove the smell and cut into pieces.
3. Heat 1 Tbsp sesame oil in a frying pan and stir-fry (1) and (2). Add seasonings (2 Tbsp shoyu, 1½ Tbsp sugar, 1 Tbsp sake, 1 chili pepper cut into pieces) and mix well.

TURNIP SEASONED WITH CITRON

Ingredients (4 servings) and method: 1. Cut 6 turnips into 6 or 8 pieces, leaving ¾" (2 cm) stems.
2. Peel the zest of ½ citron and cut into julienne strips.
3. Combine (1) and (2) in a bowl and sprinkle over salt and mix all, rubbing. If kombu is available, put it on and allow to stand for some time with a weight (ex. plate) placed on it.
4. When the whole is softened, serve in a bowl.

Dishes in a small bowl and soup go well with sushi. Prepare simple ones to save time and labor which are required to make sushi.

SIMMERED KOYA-DOFU

Ingredients (4 servings) and method: 1. Soak 4 koya-dofu (freeze-dried tofu) in water and wash by pressing. Cut in half.
2. Roll 2 fuki (butterburs) back and forth on a board sprinkled with salt. Boil and then put in water and skin. Cut into 1½" (4 cm) lengths. Boil 8 snow peas.
3. Bring 1 cup dashi stock to a boil. Add (1) and 2 Tbsp sugar, 1½ Tbsp light shoyu, 1 Tbsp sake, ¼ tsp salt, and simmer slowly. In the course of simmering add the fuki and finish up with snow peas and kinome (young leaves of Japanese pepper).

SPINACH WITH SESAME DRESSING

Ingredients (4 servings) and method: 1. Parboil ½ bunch of spinach in salted water. Drop a pinch of shoyu and squeeze out water. Cut into 1½" (4 cm) lengths.
2. Break up the petals of 3 chrysanthemum flowers. Parboil in vinegared water. Transfer to cold water immediately and squeeze out water.
3. Arrange (1) and (2) in a bowl and dress with sesame dressing (combine 4 Tbsp ground black sesame, 2 tsp miso, 2 Tbsp sugar and 1 tsp shoyu).

CUCUMBER PICKLED IN SHOYU

Ingredients (4 servings) and method: 1. Roll 3 cucumbers back and forth on a board sprinkled with salt. Make cracks by tapping with a wooden pestle. Cut into bite-sized pieces.
2. Cut 2¾" (7 cm) kombu and 1 piece ginger into julienne strips.
3. Combine (1), (2) and ⅓ oz (10 g) dried shrimps in a bowl. Add 4 Tbsp shoyu and mix well.
4. When well seasoned, serve on a plate.

KIBINAGO DRESSED WITH VINEGARED MISO

Ingredients (4 servings) and method: 1. Wash 5¼ oz (150 g) kibinago (round herring) in salted water and drain.
2. Cut 1 udo into rectangles and put into vinegared water. Parboil ½ bunch of rape blossoms in salted water. Drop pinch shoyu and squeeze out water. Cut into 1½" (4 cm) lengths.
3. Prepare vinegared miso by combining 2 Tbsp each of miso and vinegar, 2 tsp each of mirin and mustard. Dress (1) and (2) with vinegared miso and serve in a bowl topped with mustard.

KAMABOKO SOUP (p. 25)

Ingredients (4 servings) and method: 1. Cut the kamaboko (boiled fish paste) into 8 slices, each ¼" (7 mm) thick.
2. Parboil ¼ bunch of rape blossoms in salted water. Transfer immediately to cold water and squeeze out water. Cut into 1½" (4 cm) lengths.
3. Bring 4 cups dashi stock to a boil in a pot. Season with 1 tsp each of salt and light shoyu. Add (1) and (2) and bring to a boil. Serve in a bowl.

KAKITAMA-JIRU (Beaten Egg Soup) (p. 32)

Ingredients (4 servings) and method: 1. Beat 2 eggs lightly. Cut 8 mitsuba (honewort) into ¾" (2cm) lengths.
2. Bring 4 cups dashi stock to a boil in a pot. Season with 1 Tbsp sake, 1 tsp salt, 2 tsp light shoyu. Pour in beaten eggs gradually, stirring lightly.
3. When the eggs are set, transfer to a bowl and top with the mitsuba.
★If you desire, you may add starch-water mixture to thicken before the beaten eggs. (Dissolve starch with an equal portion of water.)

CHRYSANTHEMUM-EGG SOUP (p. 37)

Ingredients (4 servings) and method: 1. Cut a sheet of square thin omelet into 4 equal parts. Make slits at intervals of ⅛" (5 mm) without cutting through. Fold in half and roll up (petals of chrysanthemum). In this way make 4 pieces.
2. Soak 8 fu (dried wheat gluten) in water. Parboil snow peas in salted water.
3. Bring 1 cup dashi stock to a boil in a pot. Season with 1 tsp each of salt and light shoyu. Add (1) and (2) and bring to a boil and serve in a bowl.

WHITE FISH & OKRA SOUP

Ingredients (4 servings) and method: 1. Cut each of 2 white fish fillets into 4 pieces. Pour boiled water over.
2. Sprinkle 4 okras with salt and parboil. Cut into ring slices.
3. Bring 4 cups dashi stock to a boil in a pot. Add (1) and bring to a boil. Season with 1 Tbsp sake and 1 tsp each of salt and light shoyu. Add (2), warm up and serve in a bowl.

SHRIMP-BALL SOUP

Ingredients (4 servings) and method: 1. Ground 8 shrimps to a paste. Add 1 Tbsp egg white, 2 Tbsp cornstarch, 1 tsp sake, dash ginger juice and salt. Divide into 8 portions and form each into a ball and cook in boiling water.
2. Separate ½ pack enoki mushrooms into pieces.
3. Bring 4 cups dashi stock to a boil in a pot. Add (1) and (2) and bring to a boil. Season with 1 tsp each of salt and light shoyu and serve in a bowl. Top with kinome (young leaves of Japanese pepper).

CHICKEN BREAST & MUSHROOM SOUP

Ingredients (4 servings) and method: 1. Remove strings from 2 chicken breasts. Slice diagonally into bite-sized chunks.
2. Cut away root clusters of ½ pack shimeji mushrooms, and separate.
3. Bring 4 cups of dashi stock to a boil. Add (1) and (2) and parboil. Season with 1 tsp each of salt and light shoyu and serve in a bowl. Flavor with a piece of citron zest.

CLAM SOUP

Ingredients (4 servings) and method: 1. Soak 12 hard-shell clams in salted water to let them expel sand. Wash well, rubbing shells with a brush.
2. Parboil 1⅖ oz (40 g) barilla.
3. Place 4 cups dashi stock and clams in a pot. Bring to a boil and then lower heat. When clams open, season with 1⅓ tsp salt. Add the barilla and bring to a boil and serve in a bowl.

YUBA & SHIITAKE SOUP

Ingredients (4 servings) and method: 1. Pour boiled water over 4 pieces raw yuba (sheets of dried soybean casein).
2. Remove the stems of 2 shiitake mushrooms. Cut the caps in quarters.
3. Tie each 2 stalks of 8 mitsuba (honewort).
4. Bring 4 cups dashi stock to a boiling. Add (1) and (2) and bring to a boiling. Season with 1 tsp each of salt and light shoyu and serve in a bowl topped with the mitsuba.

GARNISHES FOR SUSHI

WASABI HORSERADISH

●The pungent aroma and pleasing sharp taste go very well with fish and it is indispensable to sushi. The best wasabi has a thick stalk. Any remaining after use should be kept in the refrigerator in plastic wrap.

●Remove the leaves and shave off the hard parts of the leafy end. Don't pare, but scrape off the rugged surface. Starting with the leafy end, grate it on a grater which has a fine abrasive surface. Always use freshly grated wasabi.

AMAZU-SHOUGA
(Sweet-vinegared Ginger)

●The sweet-sour and spicy taste is an indispensable accent to sushi. It is an excellent antidote for food poisoning and simple and easy to make. It keeps well, so you had better prepare a somewhat larger quantity. You may add umezu (plum vinegar) if you like.

Ingredients (4~5 ginger pieces) and method: 1. Cut the ginger into thin slices. Sprinkle with salt and soften.
2. Blanch in boiling water and soak in amazu (bring 1 cup vinegar, 2⅘ oz (80 g) suger and 2 tsp salt to a boil and let cool).

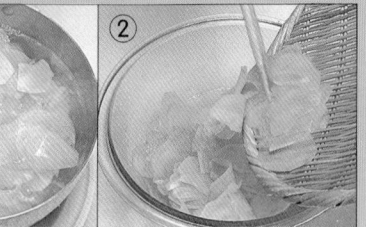

KIKKA AMAZU-ZUKE
(Sweet-vinegared Chrysanthemum)

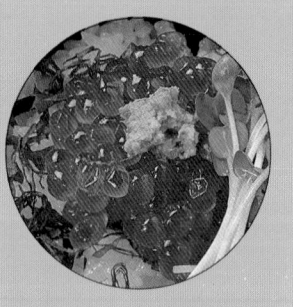

●A slightly bitter taste and vivid color are valuable for sushi like amazu-shouga. Even a violet chrysanthemum is good for variety. Prepare a somewhat larger quantity so that you can make colorful baked fish and food in sweetened vinegar.

Ingredients (3½ oz (100 g) chrysanthemum blossoms) and method:
1. Break up petals of the chrysanthemum. Blanch in vinegared boiling water and transfer to cold water.
2. Drain and soak in amazu (bring 1 cup vinegar, 2⅘ oz (80 g) suger and 2 tsp salt to a boil and let cool).

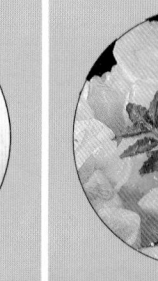

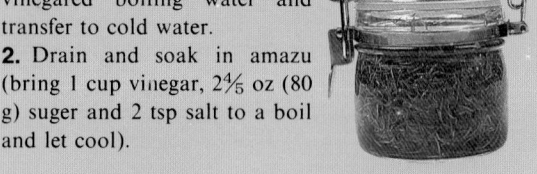

KINOME

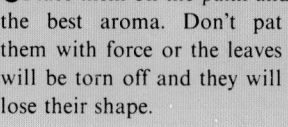

●Kinome is young leaves of Japanese pepper. The refreshing aroma and a little pungent taste are characteristics of kinome. When used with raw seafood, they diminish fishy smell and make the food savory. They also have an excellent detoxification effect.

●Place them on the palm and pat lightly to bring out the best aroma. Don't pat them with force or the leaves will be torn off and they will lose their shape.

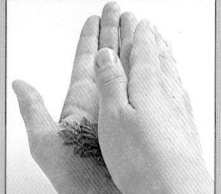

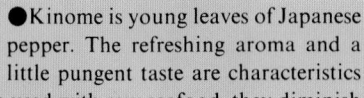